Of Thee I Sing!

A Celebration of America's Music for 2-Part Choirs

by Sally K. Albrecht and Jay Althouse
Recording Produced by Alan Billingsley

Musical Sequence

Reproducible Student Pages and Staging Included!

Performance time: approximately 30 minutes.
See back cover for CD Track Numbers.

ISBN-10: 0-7390-4657-8 (Book)
ISBN-13: 978-0-7390-4657-9 (Book)
ISBN-10: 0-7390-4658-6 (CD)
ISBN-13: 978-0-7390-4658-6 (CD)
ISBN-10: 0-7390-4659-4 (Book/CD Kit)
ISBN-13: 978-0-7390-4659-3 (Book/CD Kit)

Cover Illustration by Charles Grace.

Foreword

For several years, classroom and choral directors have been approaching me at conventions and reading sessions inquiring if I had written a patriotic program. So, to those of you who asked and encouraged me to do this, thank you!

I felt that the most difficult thing to do was to come up with a concept that included all styles of music, all races, all religions, all creeds, and yet covered much of America's past, without a heavy discussion of wars and conflicts. Then it hit me: what better way to celebrate America than through the incredible history of its music?

This program or mini-musical is designed to be flexible. The selections may all be performed by a single group, or if you have many classrooms you may have all of your singers perform the opening and closing number, then split up the other selections between multiple classes. You may also wish to feature small groups, duets, or even soloists on all or part of several selections. Variety is always a plus in any kind of programming.

This production features narrations for 50 students. The director may certainly reduce that number by doubling up on lines. Or only two narrators may be used (one doing even lines, one doing odd lines), or delete the narration and simply use this publication as a beginning 2-part songbook.

Feel free to add additional appropriate selections (perhaps a current pop ballad or hip-hop number towards the end of the program) in order to show more diversity.

Staging Notes

The staging written in above the choral parts has been designed to be performed on choral risers. You'll see that I focused primarily on upper torso movement. Please note: when movement is only written above the Part I music staff, then all voices should do that movement in unison. But when staging notes appear above both vocal staves, then the movement matches each of the individual vocal lines.

Two of these titles are available on our Alfred movement DVDs.

4. Elijah and Joshua — demonstrated on the ON WITH THE SHOW! DVD #27435.

6. A Cohan Salute — demonstrated in a longer choral version (entitled "A Patriotic Salute!") on the STEP BY STEP DVD #27431.

Again, flexibility is the key. Not every student has to do the staging for every number. Feature small groups, quartets, or trios downstage in front of the choral group.

Enjoy exploring the variety and history of musical styles in *Of Thee I Sing!*

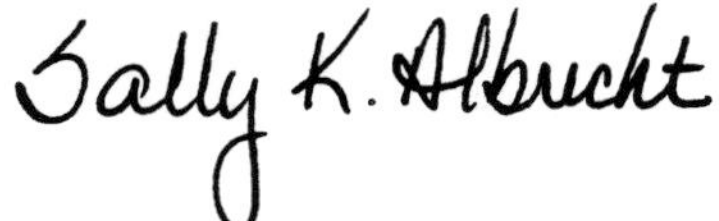

About the Composers

Sally K. Albrecht

Sally K. Albrecht is the Director of School Choral and Classroom Publications for Alfred Publishing. She is a popular choral conductor, composer, and clinician, especially known for her work with choral movement. Sally has over 300 popular choral publications, songbooks, musicals, and cantatas in print. She has produced several choral movement videos and recently compiled and edited Alfred's popular sourcebook, *The Choral Warm-Up Collection.*

Jay Althouse

Jay Althouse received a B.S. degree in Music Education and a M.Ed. degree in Music from Indiana University of Pennsylvania. As a composer of choral music, Mr. Althouse has over 500 works in print for choirs of all levels. He is the co-writer of two best-selling Alfred books, *The Complete Choral Warm-Up Book* and *Accent on Composers*. Most recently, he completed a reproducible sequential text on music reading readiness entitled *Ready to Read Music*.

Sally and Jay currently enjoy living in Raleigh, North Carolina.

About the Recording

Of Thee I Sing! was recorded at Noteworthy Studios — Manhattan Beach, CA
Alan Billingsley — Producer

Jay Althouse, Alan Billingsley, John O'Reilly, and Steve Herold — Instrumental Arrangers

Performers Include:

Connor Berkompas, Curtis Berkompas, Allie Hernandez, Ally Van Deuren, Grace Walker

alfred.com

Visit the Alfred website for more information on all of Alfred's elementary musicals, programs, songbooks, and classroom resources.

Here are the singers or vocal groups who recorded the songs mentioned in *Rock 'n' Roll Party Tonight.* We're sure your students would enjoy experiencing some or all of these recordings.

Long Tall Sally - Little Richard
Duke of Earl - Gene Chandler
Johnny B. Goode - Chuck Barry
Surfer Girl - The Beach Boys
Leader of the Pack - The Shangri-Las
Peggy Sue - Buddy Holly
Good Golly, Miss Molly - Little Richard
Hey, Hey Paula - Paul and Paula
Louie, Louie - The Kingsmen
Judy's Turn to Cry - Lesley Gore
My Boyfriend's Back - The Angels
Fun, Fun, Fun - The Beach Boys
You Can't Hurry Love - The Supremes
Still the One - Orleans
Respect - Aretha Franklin
Save the Last Dance for Me - The Drifters
I Heard It Through the Grapevine - Marvin Gaye
Dancing in the Street - Martha and the Vandellas
Tossin' and Turnin' - Bobby Lewis
Teen Beat - Sandy Nelson
You Talk Too Much - Joe Jones
(Remember) Walkin' in the Sand - The Shangri-Las
One Fine Day - The Chiffons
I Want to Hold Your Hand - The Beatles

1. OF THEE I SING, AMERICA!

Words by SALLY K. ALBRECHT
and JAY ALTHOUSE

Music by
JAY ALTHOUSE

10
R
L
R arm circle pan
mer - i - ca,
from sea to shin - ing sea.
mer - i - ca,
from sea to shin - ing sea.
13
14
Open stance w/arms behind
Slow look across from high R to high L
mf
From snow-capped moun - tain rang - es
mf
16
mf
Look across from L to R
to o-ceans white with foam.
From the Col - o - ra - do plain to the
From the Col - o - ra - do plain to the

19
Cross fists front at chest
Open palms and drop
rock - y coast of Maine, this is the land we call home.
rock - y coast of Maine, this is the land we call home.
22
March
R L R L
R palm over heart
Of thee I sing, A - mer - i - ca. My coun - try 'tis of
Of thee I sing, A - mer - i - ca. My coun - try 'tis of
25
March
R L R L
thee. Of thee I sing, A - mer - i - ca,
thee. Of thee I sing, A - mer - i - ca,

28
R arm circle pan
from sea to shin - ing sea.
from sea to shin - ing sea.
Open stance facing R diagonal
31
A bit faster
mf
My coun - try 'tis of thee, sweet land of
mf
My coun - try 'tis of thee, sweet land of
A bit faster
mf
34
lib - er - ty, of thee I sing.
lib - er - ty, of thee I sing.

37
R palm over heart
Land where my fa - thers died.
Land of the
Land where my fa - thers died.
Land of the
40
R salute, facing front
Pil - grim's pride.
From ev - 'ry
Pil - grim's pride.
From ev - 'ry
42
Push R up
cresc.
Drop to R
poco rit.
moun - tain - side let free - dom ring.
cresc.
moun - tain - side let free - dom ring.
3
cresc.
poco rit.
3

45
Tempo I
DESCANT
March forward
R L R L
R salute
Push R up
A - mer - i - ca,
Tempo I
March in place
I.
R L R L
R palm over heart
Of thee I sing, A - mer - i - ca. My coun - try 'tis of
II.
Of thee I sing, A - mer - i - ca. My coun - try 'tis of
Tempo I
Drop to R
48
of thee I sing.
March back
R L R L
(end Descant, rejoin section)
thee.
March in place
R L R L
Of thee I sing, A - mer - i - ca,
thee.
Of thee I sing, A - mer - i - ca,

51
R arm circle pan
from sea to shin - ing sea.
From sea to
from sea to shin - ing sea.
From sea to
53
Divide into 4 groups
1. Salute
2.
54
3.
4.
shin - ing sea.
Push R up and drop to R
R salute
From sea to
March
R L R L
shin - ing,
of thee I sing, A - mer - i - ca.
57
Push R up and drop to R
sea.
both parts:
Open stance
rit.
ff
Lift R up
R salute
A - mer - i - ca.
R L
Of thee I sing,
A - mer - i - ca.
8va
8vb

NARRATOR 1:

American music is a mixture of the traditions of its people. Americans come from many cultures, and so does their music.

NARRATOR 2:

Our music reflects the history of America's people, America's trials, and America's growth.

NARRATOR 3:

The music of the American Indian includes legends, songs, and dances, rich in tradition and vital to our American heritage.

NARRATOR 4:

In the Navajo tribe, it was believed that if someone was sick, his spirit should journey to a holy place beyond the sacred mountain, where it could be healed.

NARRATOR 5:

But you could move most swiftly if you made this journey on a rainbow.

2. I MOVE SWIFTLY WITH THE RAINBOW

Words and Music by
SALLY K. ALBRECHT *and* **JAY ALTHOUSE**

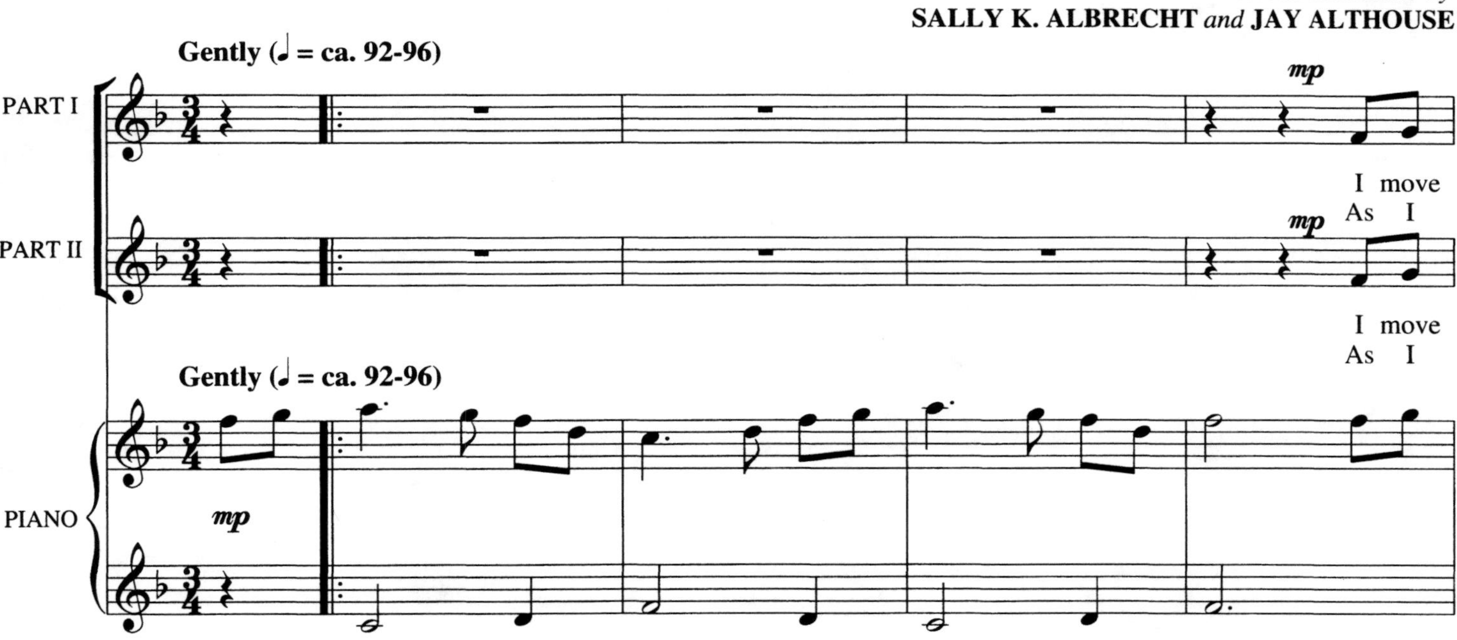

Translation/Pronunciation Guide
Hee yah hoh, (vocables)
bee-keh hoh-shawn, (happiness in all things)
sah ah-nah-reye, (life unending)
hee yah heh. (vocables)

NOTE: Verse 1 and Verse 2 may be performed by soloists. All join in on Chorus.

5
swift - ly with the rain - bow to the moun - tains far a - bove. As I trav - el I think
jour - ney, I grow wea - ry, for my way is rough and steep. But the rain - bow moves me
swift - ly with the rain - bow to the moun - tains far a - bove. As I trav - el I think
jour - ney, I grow wea - ry, for my way is rough and steep. But the rain - bow moves me
mf
13
fond - ly of the peo - ple that I love. Hi ya ho, bi - ke ho - shon, sa a -
swift - ly, miles to go be - fore I sleep.
mf
fond - ly of the peo - ple that I love. Hi ya ho, bi - ke ho - shon, sa a -
swift - ly, miles to go be - fore I sleep.
mf
na - rai, hi ya he. Hi ya ho, bi - ke ho - shon, hi ya he.
na - rai, hi ya he. Hi ya ho, bi - ke ho - shon, hi ya he.

NARRATOR 6:
Songs give people a common bond, which was especially important as America began to grow.

NARRATOR 7:
New songs were improvised and passed down. Songs of the common people—cowboys, farmers, railroad men, sailors, and lumberjacks.

NARRATOR 8:
This music was used to play games, to dance, to put children to sleep, to establish a working tempo.

NARRATOR 9:
These songs reflected the spirit of the common folk, and became known as American Folk Songs.

3. FOLK SONG MEDLEY

Arranged by
JAY ALTHOUSE

5
In a flowing manner (♩ = ca. 108-112)
wide, I can-not cross o'er. And nei-ther have
In a flowing manner (♩ = ca. 108-112)
9
(opt. solo 2) mp
I the wings to fly. Build me a
13
boat that can car - ry two, and both shall
17
(end solo)
PART I
mp
row, my love and I. I leaned my
cresc.

21
PART I
mf
back on a fine young oak.
PART II
mf
I leaned my back on a fine young
mf
24
I thought it was a trust - y tree.
oak. I thought it was a trust - y
28
29
But first it bend - ed and then it broke.
tree. But first it bend - ed and then it broke.

32
mp
Thus did my love prove false to me.
mp
Thus did my love prove false to me.
mp
37
rit.
Oo
The wa-ter is wide.
Oo
The wa-ter is wide.
rit.
42
Brightly (𝅗𝅥 = ca. 116)
mf
You
mf
You
Brightly (𝅗𝅥 = ca. 116)
mf

46
Knee bends
down up down up etc.
ought to see my Cin - dy, she lives a - way down South. And
ought to see my Cin - dy, she lives a - way down South. And
50
Shimmer fingers at mouth
she's so sweet the hon - ey bees swarm a - round her mouth. Get a - long
she's so sweet the hon - ey bees swarm a - round her mouth. Get a - long
54
Scoop look R w/R above eyes
Scoop look L w/L above eyes
home, Cin - dy, Cin - dy, get a - long home, Cin - dy, Cin - dy. Get a - long
home, Cin - dy, Cin - dy, get a - long home, Cin - dy, Cin - dy. Get a - long

58
Scoop look front w/R above eyes
Clasp hands front
sub. p
home, Cin - dy, Cin - dy, I'll mar - ry you some - day. Get a - long
sub. p
home, Cin - dy, Cin - dy, I'll mar - ry you some - day. Get a - long
sub. p
62
Scoop look R as before
Scoop look L
home, Cin - dy, Cin - dy, get a - long home, Cin - dy, Cin - dy. Get a - long
home, Cin - dy, Cin - dy, get a - long home, Cin - dy, Cin - dy. Get a - long
66
Scoop look front
Clasp hands front
cresc.
home, Cin - dy, Cin - dy, I'll mar - ry you some -
cresc.
home, Cin - dy, Cin - dy, I'll mar - ry you some -
cresc.

69
Open hands front
Drop to sides
mf
day.
mf
day.
mf
f
73
Double time low bounce front w/hands on thighs
With spirit (♩ - ca. 116)
With spirit (♩ - ca. 116)
77
Lift R knee
and hit
hit
hit
hit
mf

81
Punch R fist across
Hit own head w/R palm
mf
Old Dan Tuck-er was a might-y good man; washed his face in a fry - ing pan.
85
Comb hair w/L fingers
Pray front
Look down L
mf
Combed his head with a wag - on wheel. Died with a tooth - ache in his heel.
89
R index points out to R
Shake it 3x
mf
Get out the way, Old Dan Tuck-er. You're too late to get your sup- per.
Get out the way, Old Dan Tuck-er. You're too late to get your sup- per.

93
Flip R palm down
Flip L palm up
Fold arms front
Sup-per's o - ver and din-ner's cook-in', and Old Dan Tuck-er
Sup-per's o - ver and din-ner's cook-in', and Old Dan Tuck-er
96
Nod head front
97
Double time low bounce w/hands on thighs
stands there look-in'.
stands there look-in'.
f
100
Scoop R
L
R
L

105
Tilt clap
R L R L
R lasso above 2x
Old Dan Tuck-er's back in town, swing-in' the la-dies all a-round.
109
Tilt clap
R L R L
R lasso above 2x
First to the right and then to the left, then to the gal that
112
113
R index points to R
Shake it 3x
Get out the way, Old Dan Tuck-er. You're too late to
he loves best. Get out the way, Old Dan Tuck-er. You're too late to

116
Flip R palm down
Flip L palm up
get your sup - per. Sup - per's o - ver and din - ner's cook - in',
get your sup - per. Sup - per's o - ver and din - ner's cook - in', and
119
Fold arms
Open arms
Fists on waist
Old Dan Tuck - er stands there
Fold arms
Old Dan Tuck - er stands there
8va
123
Scoop look R
Scoop look L
Lift R knee and hit 3x
R fist up
look - in'. Yes, sir!
look - in'. Yes, sir!

NARRATOR 10:

Spirituals were sometimes exultant, sometimes sad. They spoke of deliverance, of a journey to a better place, of seeking freedom, of hope for the future.

NARRATOR 11:

In the church, spirituals were sung in order to commune with God. There were songs of rejoicing, of prayer, of deliverance.

NARRATOR 12:

In the world outside of the church, African-Americans used spirituals to communicate. Lyrics were secret codes, telling of meetings or ways to escape.

NARRATOR 13:

Spirituals reflected years of African-American slavery, of being oppressed and in deep despair.

NARRATOR 14:

Yet, the lyrics ring of dignity, of power, of hope, faith, triumph, and rejoicing in the midst of those terrible dark times.

4. ELIJAH AND JOSHUA

Traditional Spirituals
Arranged by
SALLY K. ALBRECHT

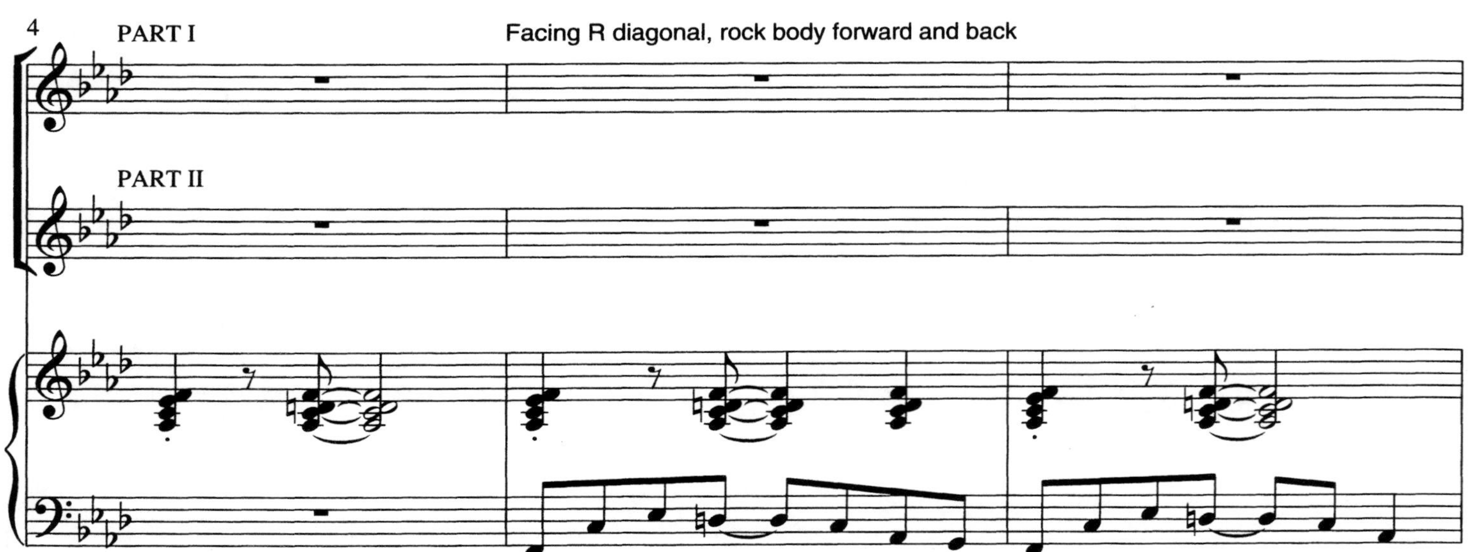

7
9
mf
Reach both out to R
E - li - jah
mf
10
mf
Reach both out to R
E - li - jah
Clasp and pull in
and
13
Clasp and pull in
Reach both out to L
and Josh - u - a.
to L
Josh - u - a.

Stomp and pull shoulders back
R L
17
Body rock
R to mouth
L to mouth
E - li - jah rock, shout, shout.
E - li - jah rock, shout, shout.
Body rock
Shimmer jazz hands around face
Body rock
E - li - jah rock, com - in' up, Lord. E - li - jah rock,
E - li - jah rock, com - in' up, Lord. E - li - jah rock,
R to mouth
L to mouth
Body rock
Push both jazz up to R
Snap 2x
shout, shout. E - li - jah rock, com - in' up,
shout, shout. E - li - jah rock, com - in' up,

25
Clasped hands circle from low R up ...
fp
cresc.
Lord
... and flip over to L and drop
Body rock
R to mouth
L to mouth
decresc.
E - li - jah rock,
shout,
shout.
E - li - jah rock,
decresc.
28
29
Reach L hand across to R
and pull into chest
mp
shout,
shout.
Rock - a my soul in the bos - om of A - bra - ham.
Rock - a my soul in the bos - om of A - bra - ham.
mp
31
w/R to L
Reach both up and cross at chest
cresc.
Rock - a my soul in the bos - om of A - bra - ham. Rock - a my soul in the
Rock - a my soul in the bos - om of A - bra - ham. Rock - a my soul in the
cresc.

Stomp and shoulders
R L
Clasped hands circle as before
34
bos-om of A - bra-ham. Rock - a my soul.
Body rock
bos-om of A - bra-ham. E - li - jah rock,
37
R to mouth
L to mouth
shout, shout. E - li - jah rock, shout, shout.
40
Stand tall
R jazz palm front
L jazz palm front
Josh-ua fit the bat-tle of Jer - i - cho, Jer - i - cho,
Josh-ua fit the bat-tle of Jer - i - cho, Jer - i - cho,

43
Push both up and fall
Stand tall
Both jazz palms front
Jer - i - cho, Josh - ua fit the bat - tle of Jer - i - cho, and the
Jer - i - cho, Josh - ua fit the bat - tle of Jer - i - cho,
46
Push up
Push up 2x
decresc.
walls come tum - ba - lin' down, tum - ba - lin'
Push up
decresc.
walls come tum - ba - lin' down, tum - ba - lin'
49
Shimmer and drop
Slowly rise
down.
down.
decresc.
mp

52
53 Low pray
f
and the
f
Mime trumpet front
Then the lamb ram sheep-horns be - gan to blow,
f
55
Mime trumpet front
trum-pets be - gan to sound.
Stand tall
Then Josh - u - a com-mand-ed the
Then Josh - u - a com-mand-ed the
58
Push R fist up
peo - ple to shout,
Both jazz up
and the walls come tum - ba - lin' down,
peo - ple to shout,
Both jazz up
walls come tum - ba - lin'

61
Push up 2x
decresc.
Shimmer and drop
— tum - ba - lin' down.
decresc.
down, tum - ba - lin' down.
decresc.
64
Slowly rise
66
Stand tall
mp
Josh - ua fit the bat - tle of
Low pray
mp
67
Push both jazz up
Shimmer and drop
Jer - i - cho,
mp Body rock
R to mouth
L to mouth
E - li - jah rock, shout, shout.

70
mf
cresc.
Josh-ua fit the bat-tle of Jer-i-cho.
Low pray
mf Body rock
cresc.
E-li-jah rock,
mf
mf
cresc.
73
R jazz front
L jazz front
R higher
L higher
f
And the walls come tum-b'lin'
R to mouth
L to mouth
f
shout, shout. And the walls come tum-b'lin'
f
76
Both way up
Drop a bit
Drop a bit
Pray low
Both jazz up
down.
down.
8va
ff
8vb

NARRATOR 15:
In the early 1900s, a new kind of music appeared on the scene—Ragtime!

NARRATOR 16:
It was characterized by a syncopated or "ragged" melody over a steady "boom chick" bass line.

NARRATOR 17:
Ragtime music rang out from pianos in dance halls, clubs, theaters, and homes all across the country.

NARRATOR 18:
Plus, many of the best-selling rolls for player-pianos were ragtime. Composers Scott Joplin and "Jelly Roll" Morton popularized the style.

NARRATOR 19:
Ragtime music influenced future American musical styles, like Dixieland and jazz.

NARRATOR 20:
Here's a Dixieland-style version of Irving Berlin's famous song from 1911 called "Alexander's Ragtime Band." Listen for all the instruments!

5. ALEXANDER'S RAGTIME BAND

Arranged, with new words and music, by
SALLY K. ALBRECHT
and **JAY ALTHOUSE**

by **IRVING BERLIN**

1st time: *PART I only*
2nd time: *PART II only*
3rd time: *Sing both parts*

5
Scoop listen w/hand to ear:
R L R L
hear, come on and hear Al - ex - an - der's Rag - time Band. Come on and
Mime playing tuba – big R arm above, L arm curved front, big knee bends
mf
Oom - pah, oom - pah. Hear the tu - ba oom - pah - pah.
9
R L R L
hear, come on and hear, it's the best band in the land. They can
Mime playing clarinet – hands front, L higher, lean forward and back
The clar - i - nets, the clar - i - nets, doo-dle- oo, doo-dle - oo, the clar - i - nets.
13
Hold "trumpet" front and tilt:
R L R L
Salute w/R
play a bu - gle call like you nev - er heard be - fore, so nat - u - ral that you want to yell for more.
Mime playing trumpet – hands at mouth, tilt R and L
3
Ra-ta-ta- ta! The bu - gle call. Ra-ta-ta- ta! The best of all.

17
both parts:
Stand tall
Punch R fist across to L
Pan R palm to R
Scoop front
That's just the best - est band what am, my hon - ey lamb. Come on a -
That's just the best - est band what am, my hon - ey lamb.
21
Place palm out:
R to R back L to L back R to R back L to L back
long, come on a - long, let me take you by the hand, up to the
Mime playing trombone – L at mouth, R "slides" w/vocal line
Ah, ah. Hear the trom - bone, ah.
25
Shake jazz hands:
up down up
man, up to the man, who's the lead - er of the
Mime playing flute – hands to R of mouth, tilt R and L
Come hear the flute. Come hear the flute. Twee-dle - dee, twee-dle -

both parts:
Sway w/flat palms front:
29
28
down
R L R L R L
band. And if you care to hear the Swa - nee Riv - er played in
dee, come hear the flute. If you hear the Swa - nee Riv - er played in
both parts:
Scoop listen w/hand to ear:
32
R L R L
rag - time, come on and hear, come on and hear Al - ex -
rag - time, come on and hear, come on and hear Al - ex -
35
(repeat twice)
37
both parts:
Bounce low 4x R to L
an - der's Rag - time Band. Come on and hear, come on and hear Al - ex -
an - der's Rag - time Band. Come on and hear, come on and hear Al - ex -
(repeat twice)

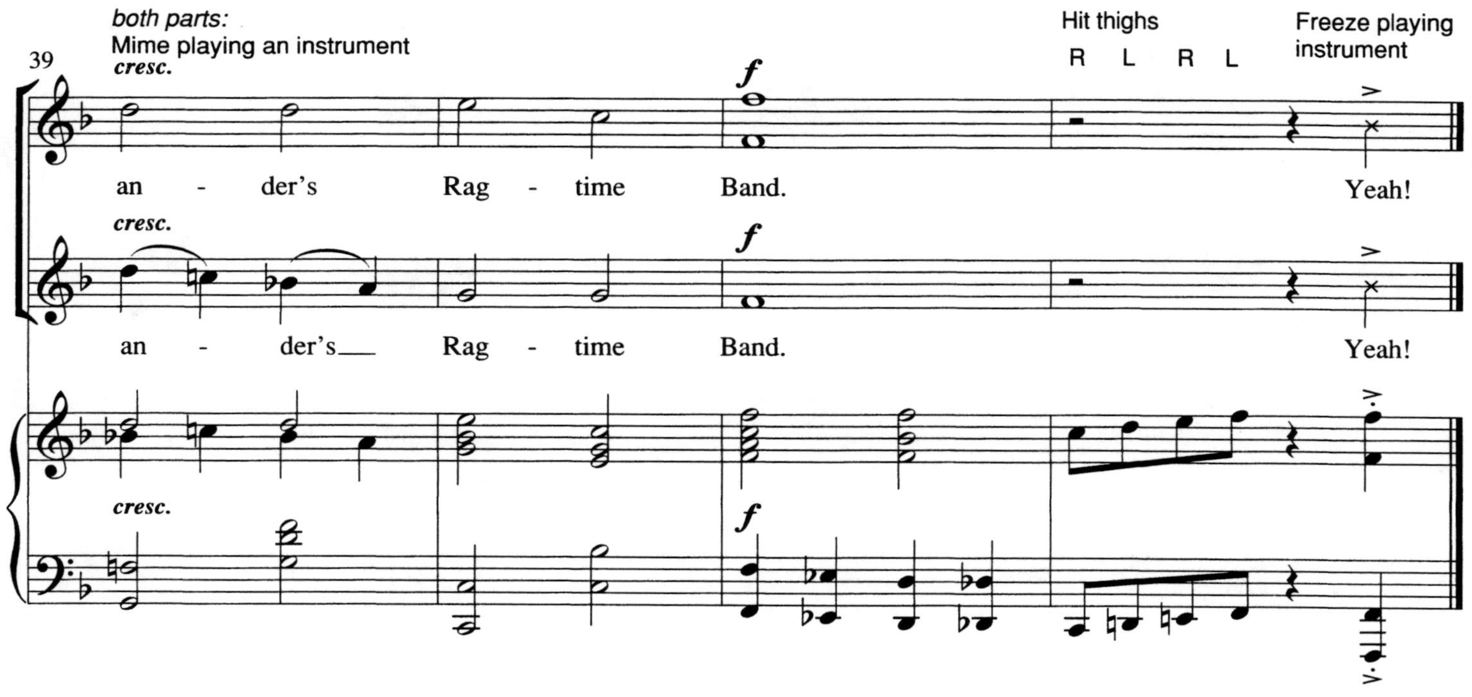

NARRATOR 21:
Meanwhile, in New York City, Broadway was hitting its golden age.

NARRATOR 22:
After years of vaudeville and music hall entertainment, the "great white way" was developing its own kind of music.

NARRATOR 23:
Music and plot were intertwined. Dramatic stories were told through both dialogue and music lyrics.

NARRATOR 24:
The time was right as George M. Cohan came onto the scene in the early 1900s with these two hit Broadway songs.

6. A COHAN SALUTE

Arranged by
SALLY K. ALBRECHT

"The Yankee Doodle Boy" by George M. Cohan

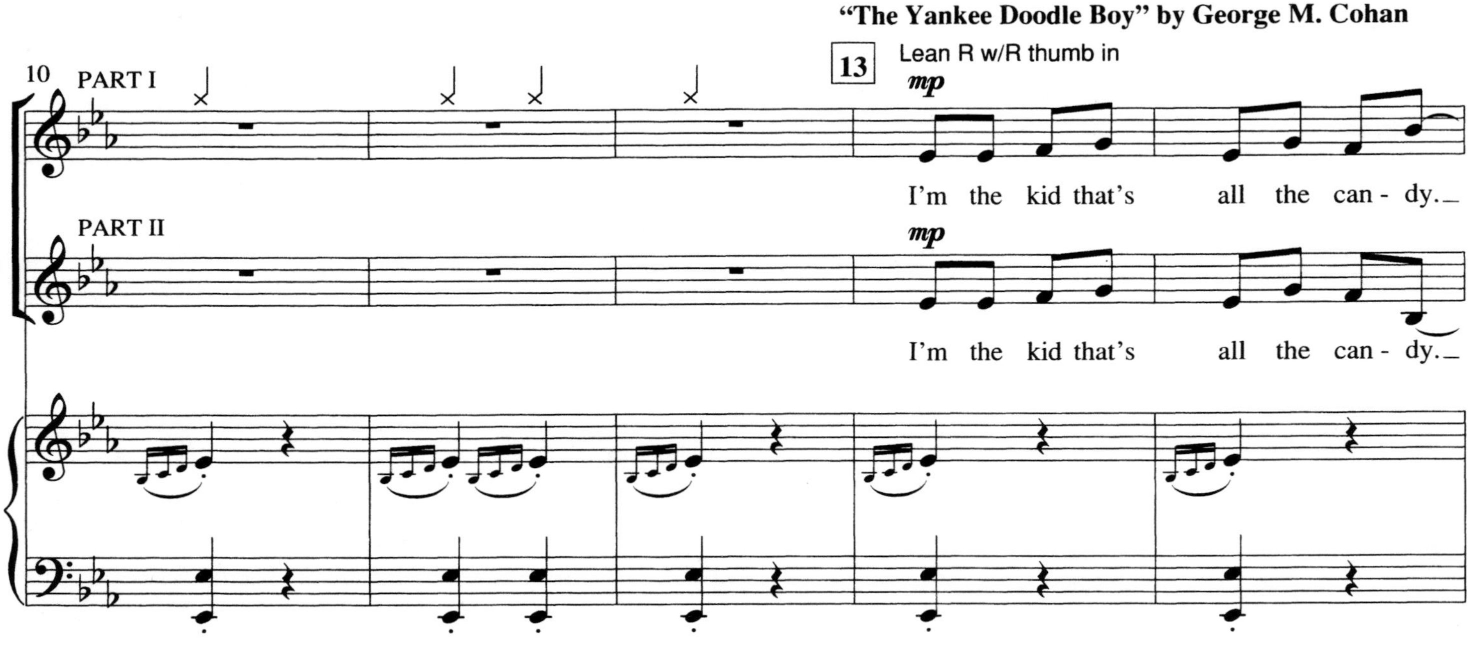

20
Both thumbs in
Point R index front
mf
(spoken)
I'm glad I am. So's Un - cle Sam!
mf
(spoken)
I'm glad I am. So's Un - cle Sam!
mp
mf
25
Bounce low 8x
I'm a real live Yan - kee Doo - dle, Made my name and fame and boo - dle,
I'm a real live Yan - kee Doo - dle, Made my name and fame and boo - dle,
29
Continue bounce, holding reins to the front
"Ride" pony facing stage L
Just like Mis - ter Doo - dle did, by rid - ing on a po - ny.
Just like Mis - ter Doo - dle did, by rid - ing on a po - ny.

Circle R arm hitting R thigh
Circle R lasso above head
41
March in place
R
L
R
L
R
I'm a Yan - kee Doo - dle Dan - dy, a Yan - kee
Ah, a Yan - kee Doo - dle, a Yan - kee

46
L
R
L
Open stance
Doo - dle, do or die.
Ah,
Doo - dle, do or die.
A real live neph - ew of my
R index point front
51
Baby rock
R
L
R
Un - cle Sam's, Born on the Fourth of Ju - ly.
Un - cle Sam's, Oh, Fourth of Ju -
56
L
57
Scoop in center w/hands clasped
I've got a Yan - kee Doo - dle sweet - heart,
ly. Ah, I've got a sweet - heart,

61
Low (get kazoo)
She's my Yan - kee Doo - dle joy.
(He's)
She's my Yan - kee Doo - dle joy.
(He's)
65
"Yankee Doodle"
Hold kazoo like trumpet front. Use elbows and knees on piano rhythm
(Kazoos or "doot")
(Kazoos or "doot")
70
Low (put kazoo away)
I am a
I am a

75
Slowly stand
Yan - kee Doo - dle boy.
Yan - kee Doo - dle boy.
Face L diagonal, R lasso above as before
"You're a Grand Old Flag" by George M. Cohan
79
f
You're a
f
You're a
83
Face R diagonal w/R hand over heart
Push R out
grand old flag, you're a high fly - ing flag, And for - ev - er in
(mel.)
grand old flag, you're a high fly - ing flag, And for - ev - er in

88
Towards flag
Open stance facing front
peace may you wave. You're the em - blem of the
peace may you wave. You're the em - blem of the
93
R salute
up
land I love, The home of the free and the brave.
land I love, The home of the free and the brave.
98
down
99
R fist
up in up in up in up in
Ev - 'ry heart beats true un - der Red, White, and Blue, Where there's
(mel.)
Ev - 'ry heart beats true un - der Red, White, and Blue, Where there's

103
Palms flat to floor
(mel.)
nev - er a boast or brag. But should auld
Scoop into group of friends
Palms flat to floor
(mel.)
nev - er a boast or brag. But should auld
108
acquain - tance be for -
Scoop into new group of friends
acquain - tance be for -
113
(mel.)
R salute
cresc.
Push up
got, Keep your eye on the grand
cresc.
got, Keep your eye on the grand
cresc.

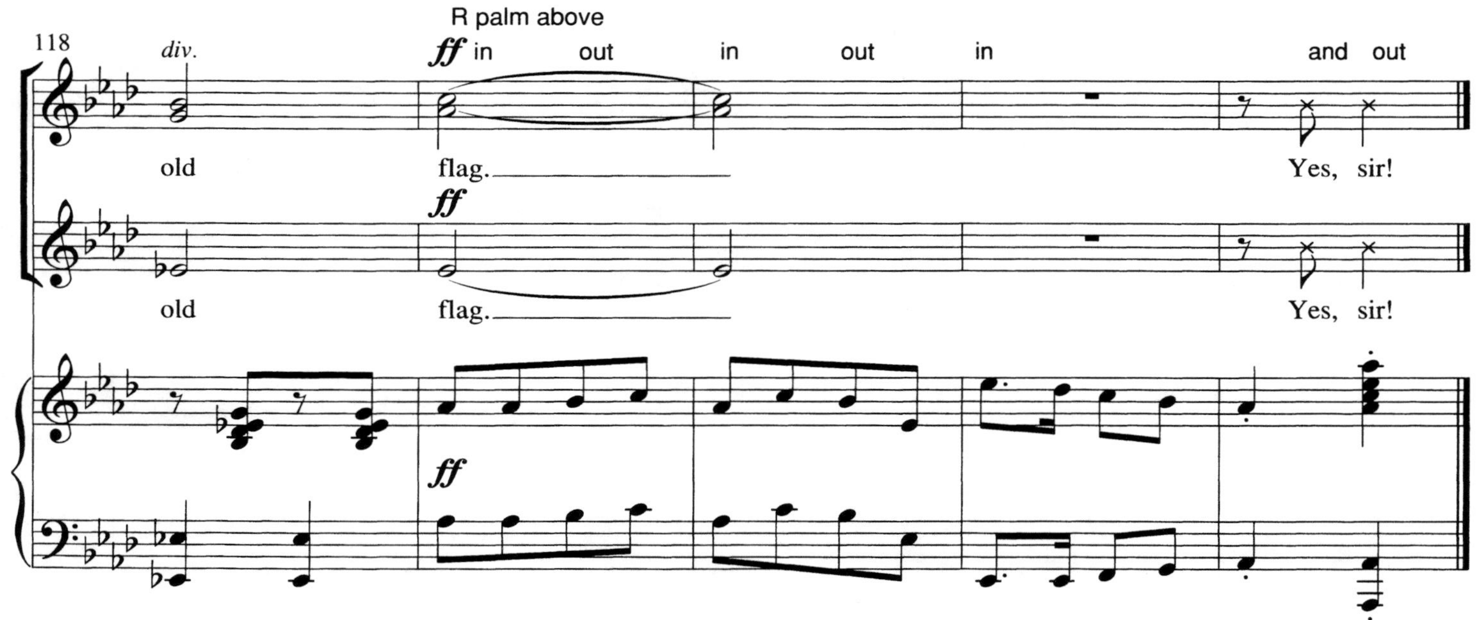

NARRATOR 25:
In the 1930s and 1940s, a new kind of music developed. Swing was king!

NARRATOR 26:
Big bands like those of Duke Ellington, Count Basie, Tommy Dorsey, and Woodie Herman played all over the world.

NARRATOR 27:
Instrumentalists like Louis Armstrong and singers like Ella Fitzgerald took this style of jazz to a new level.

NARRATOR 28:
Keep it steady. Keep it "laid back."

NARRATOR 29:
Keep tappin' those toes and poppin' those thumbs!

NARRATOR 30:
We're gonna "swing the night away!"

7. SWINGIN' THE NIGHT AWAY

Words and Music by
JAY ALTHOUSE

5
1. R toe out and in w/head
2. R fist out and in w/head
PART I mf
1. When the band starts swing-in' the beat, makes me feel like
2. Swing that beat with rhy-thm and drums. Makes me feel like
PART II mf
1. When the band starts swing-in' the beat, makes me feel like
2. Swing that beat with rhy-thm and drums. Makes me feel like
8
Palms flat to floor
R plams hold tray over R shoulder
tap-pin' my feet.
snap-pin' my thumbs.
Noth-in' could be fin-er than din-ner in a din-er, or
tap-pin' my feet.
snap-pin' my thumbs.
Noth-in' could be fin-er than din-ner in a din-er, or
1. Swing snap
2. Swing snap
11
R L R L
R L
swing-in' the night a-way.
swing-in' the night a-way.
swing-in' the night a-way.
swing-in' the night a-way.
1.
2.

14
R
L
15
Conduct w/R
Ba - sie swung it when El - la sung it. It
Sing into microphone
Ba - sie swung it when El - la sung it. It
17
Finger digs in air
al - ways sound - ed fine.
Fans all dig it and
al - ways sound - ed fine.
Fans all dig it and
20
R index point from L to R
mf
cool cats gig it. Swing it on down the line.
mf
cool cats gig it. Swing it on down the line.

23
R toe out and in w/head
When the band starts swing - in' the beat,
makes me feel like
When the band starts swing - in' the beat,
makes me feel like
26
Palms flat to floor
R tray over R shoulder
tap - pin' my feet.
Noth - in' could be fin - er than din - ner in a din - er, or
tap - pin' my feet.
Noth - in' could be fin - er than din - ner in a din - er, or
Swing snap
29
R
L
R
L
f
Snaps 8x from L to R
swing - in' the night a - way,
just swing - in' the
f
swing - in' the night a - way,
just swing - in' the
f

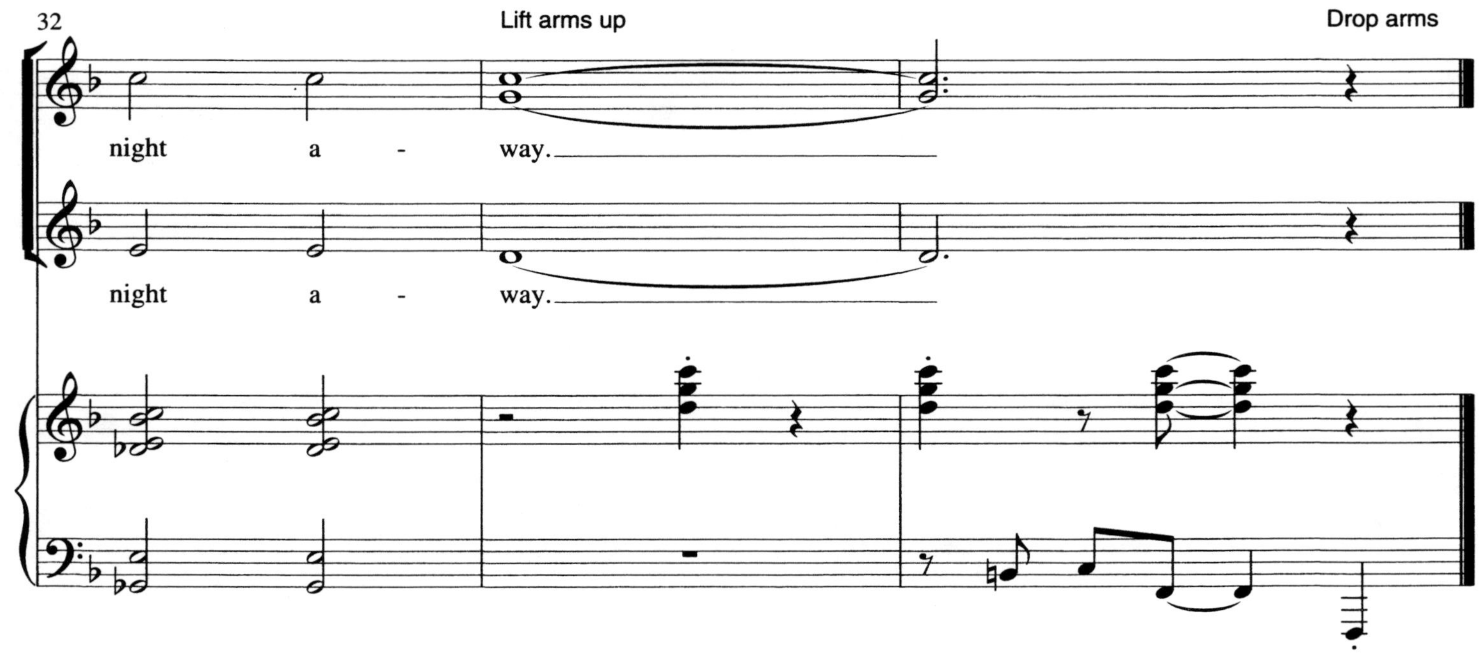

NARRATOR 31:
"Country Music" originated in the southern United States in the mid 1920s. It has its roots in a combination of folk music, Celtic music, blues, and gospel music.

NARRATOR 32:
Jimmie Rodgers and the Carter Family are commonly acknowledged as the founders of country music.

NARRATOR 33:
Many different kinds of country music have developed and still exist today, including the "Nashville sound," bluegrass, traditional western cowboy songs, country swing, jug bands, and Cajun-style Zydeco music.

NARRATOR 34:
And most of the big names have appeared on one very famous show, which has been broadcast every Saturday night continuously from Nashville, Tennessee, since November 28, 1925.

NARRATOR 35:
What began as radio's "WSM Barn Dance" was renamed in 1927 as "The Grand Ole Opry."

NARRATOR 36:
From Roy Rogers to Gene Autry, from Johnny Cash to Ray Charles,...

NARRATOR 37:
...from Elvis Presley to Vince Gill, from Patsy Cline to Dolly Parton,...

NARRATOR 38:
...from Alison Krauss to Garth Brooks, from Willie Nelson to Reba McEntire, country music has produced an incredible string of famous entertainers.

8. MAKE MINE COUNTRY

Words and Music by
SALLY K. ALBRECHT *and* **JAY ALTHOUSE**

13
Stand tall
Push neck out
R center L
need a song, make mine coun - try.
up and say: make mine coun - try.
mf Stand
If there's a
If it's the
17
Bounce low facing singers
Place L elbow on neighbor's R shoulder
good - time mel - o - dy, and you're in the key of G and you
hap - py month of June, and you need a song to croon, and you're
21
Stand
mf
Stand tall
Push neck out
R center L
Make mine
need some har - mo - ny, make mine coun - try. Make mine
look - in' for a tune, make mine coun - try.

25
Dip sway
R
L
R
L
coun - try, make mine coun - try. A
coun - try, make mine coun - try. A
29
Bounce low
Get higher 3x
coun - try song can real - ly make me smile. Make mine
coun - try song can real - ly make me smile. Make mine
33
Dip sway
R
L
R
L
coun - try, make mine coun - try. I'll take
coun - try, make mine coun - try. I'll take

37
Punch R fist across
Clap high to L
Front row do-si-do or swing a partner while back rows clap
2nd time to Coda
coun - try mu - sic (clap) mile af - ter mile.
coun - try mu - sic (clap) mile af - ter mile.
2nd time to Coda
42
mf
If it's the
CODA
47
Look from L to R w/R above eyes
Punch R fist across
Clap high to L
f
mile. I'll take coun - try mu - sic (clap) mile af - ter
f
mile. I'll take coun - try mu - sic (clap) mile af - ter
CODA
f

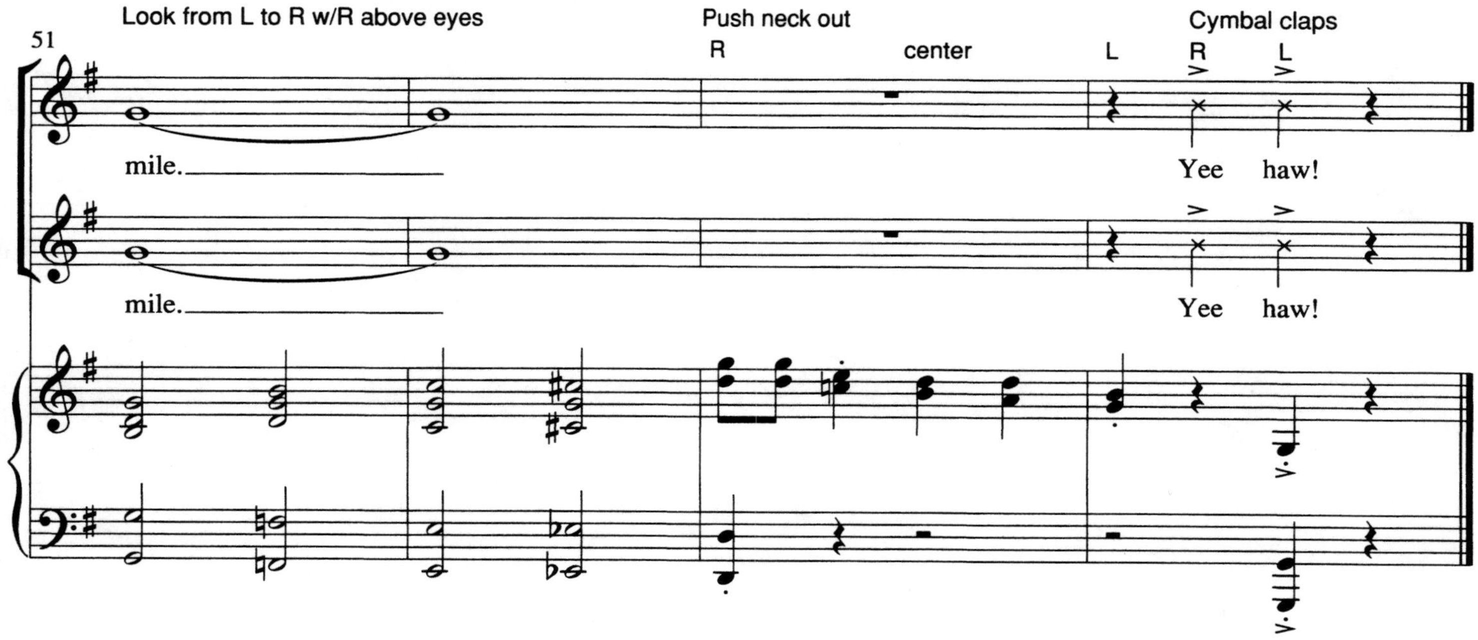

NARRATOR 39:
Since the mid 1950s, rock 'n' roll music has been one of the most popular forms of music in the world.

NARRATOR 40:
Alan Freed, a disc jockey from Cleveland, Ohio, is credited with coining the phrase "rock and roll."

NARRATOR 41:
Rock and roll combines elements of blues, soul, boogie-woogie, and jazz music.

NARRATOR 42:
The heart of rock and roll comes from the rhythm, which features a strong back beat, usually played on the snare drum.

NARRATOR 43:
So see how many song titles YOU recognize, at our "rock and roll party tonight!"

9. ROCK 'N' ROLL PARTY TONIGHT!

Rock tempo (♩ = ca. 152-160)

Words and Music by
JAY ALTHOUSE

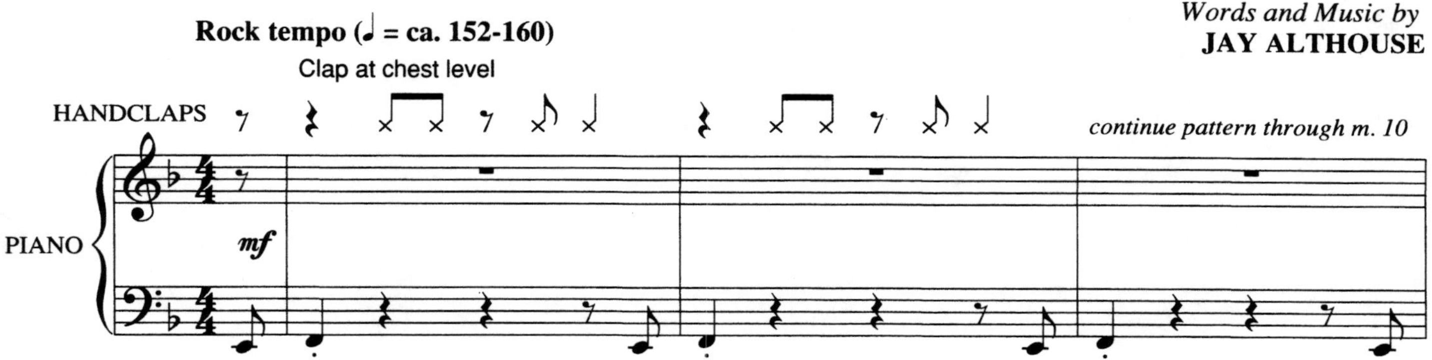

4
PART I
mf
5
Gather into "car(s)" w/driver
We were cruis - in' 'round town last Sat - ur - day night, my
PART II
mf
We were cruis - in' 'round town last Sat - ur - day night, my
7
Walk out from "car(s)"
bud - dies and me; we were look - in' all right. We went to the dance, and when we
bud - dies and me; we were look - in' all right. We went to the dance, and when we
(Handclaps)
Freeze
Shake jazz hands to center
END HANDCLAPS
10
f
o - pened the door, we saw a rock 'n' roll par - ty on the dance floor. There was
f
o - pened the door, we saw a rock 'n' roll par - ty on the dance floor. There was
f

13
Pony
R
L
Muscles facing L
Playing guitar
Long, Tall Sal-ly and the Duke of Earl,
John-ny B. Goode and his
Long, Tall Sal-ly and the Duke of Earl,
John-ny B. Goode and his
16
Surf
Ride motorcycle
Wave front
Surf-er Girl. The Lead-er of the Pack came with Peg-gy Sue. Good
Surf-er Girl. The Lead-er of the Pack came with Peg-gy Sue. Good
19
Hold face
Shake jazz hands to center
21
Low
Gol-ly, Miss Mol-ly was e-ven there, too.
Pony
R
L
Gol-ly, Miss Mol-ly was e-ven there, too. Hey, hey Pau-la and

* Pronounced "Lou-ee, Lou-eye."

31
Fold arms – mad
Reach front
Low
can't hur - ry love, but you're still the one.
Low
Fists on waist – yell forward
How a - bout some R - E - S - P -
34
Palms out at sides
Boogie!
On - ly if you save the last dance for me.
Low
E - C - T?
CODA
37
Monkey 4x R
Monkey 4x L
f
39
R to R ear
I heard it through the grape-vine you were
mf
Low
Oo
CODA

40
Swing hips and snap
R
L
R and hold
danc - in' in the street and toss - in' and a - turn - in' to the teen beat.
wah oo You
43
Low
f All low
One fine day I want to
Fists on waist
Hug self
talk too much; re - mem - ber walk - in' in the sand? One fine day I want to
46
R jazz out front, shimmer and raise each measure
hold your hand.
hold your hand, hold your hand, hold your hand.

50
Small group as before, others clap front
49
OPT. HANDCLAPS
continue pattern through m. 54
Woo! Long, Tall Sal - ly and the Duke of Earl,
Woo! Long, Tall Sal - ly and the Duke of Earl,
52
John - ny B. Goode and his Surf - er Girl. The Lead - er of the Pack came with
John - ny B. Goode and his Surf - er Girl. The Lead - er of the Pack came with
55
Hold face
Shake jazz hands to center
END HANDCLAPS
Peg - gy Sue. Good Gol - ly, Miss Mol - ly was e - ven there, too.
Peg - gy Sue. Good Gol - ly, Miss Mol - ly was e - ven there, too.

58
Low
R flat palm forward
Look out now, 'cause it's
Pony
R
L
Hitch 4x w/R
Low
Hey, hey Pau - la and Lou - ie, Lou - ie.
61
Cry to R w/R
Swing hips and snap
R
L
R
L
Ju - dy's turn to cry.
Come on ev - 'ry - bod - y, it's a rock 'n' roll par - ty.
64
Low
All swing hips and snap
R
L
Come on ev - 'ry - bod - y, it's a
Swing hips and snap
R
L
R
L
Come on ev - 'ry - bod - y, it's a rock 'n' roll par - ty.
Come on ev - 'ry - bod - y, it's a

NARRATOR 44:
The history of American music is truly varied and amazing.

NARRATOR 45:
Each style is unique in its own way, but is rooted in the history of the American people.

NARRATOR 46:
New styles are still being developed. In the late 20th and early 21st century, rap and hip-hop have been embraced by the American music scene.

NARRATOR 47:
From Native American Indian chants to traditional folk songs,...

NARRATOR 48:
... from inspirational spirituals to hot New Orleans ragtime,...

NARRATOR 49:
... from jazzy swing to kickin' Broadway 2-beat,...

NARRATOR 50:
... from Nashville's Grand Ole Opry to the Detroit Motown Sound,...

ALL:
... America has developed a sound all its own.

10. FINALE: OF THEE I SING, AMERICA!

Words by SALLY K. ALBRECHT
and JAY ALTHOUSE

Music by
JAY ALTHOUSE

12
Push R up
cresc.
Drop to R
poco rit.
moun - tain - side let free - dom ring.
cresc.
moun - tain - side let free - dom ring.
cresc.
poco rit.
Majestically (♩ = ca. 84-88)
DESCANT
15
March forward
R L R L
R salute
Push R up
A - mer - i - ca,
Tempo I
March in place
I.
R L R L
R palm over heart
Of thee I sing, A - mer - i - ca. My coun-try 'tis of
II.
Of thee I sing, A - mer - i - ca. My coun-try 'tis of
Majestically (♩ = ca. 84-88)

3

18 Drop to R

March back

R L R L

(end Descant, rejoin section)

of thee I sing.

March in place

R L R L

thee. Of thee I sing, A - mer - i - ca,

thee. Of thee I sing, A - mer - i - ca,

24
3.
4.
Push R up and drop to R
R salute
shin - ing sea.
From sea to
March
R L R L
shin - ing,
Of thee I sing, A - mer - i - ca.
Push R up and drop to R
both parts:
Open stance
Lift R up
R salute
27
rit.
ff
sea.
A - mer - i - ca.
R L
Of thee I sing,
A - mer - i - ca.
8va
8vb

REPRODUCIBLE STUDENT PAGES

1. OF THEE I SING, AMERICA!

Words by **SALLY K. ALBRECHT**
and **JAY ALTHOUSE**

Music by
JAY ALTHOUSE

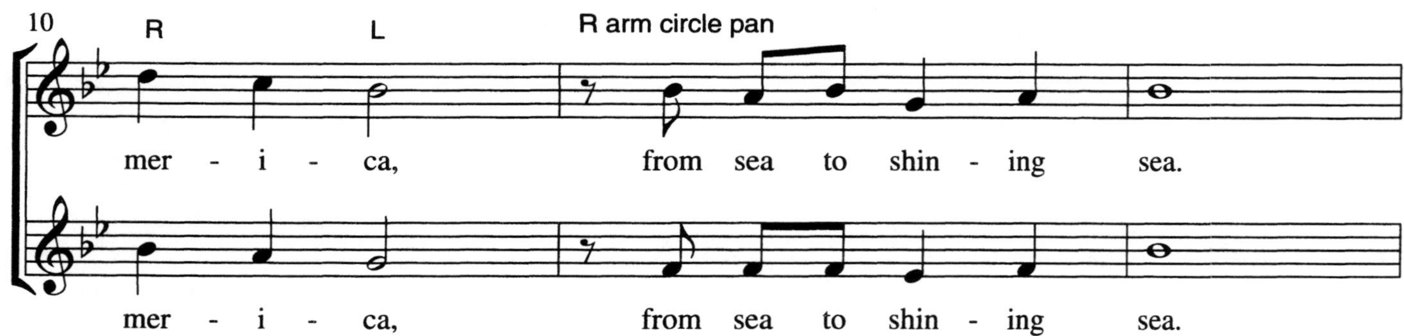

13
14
Open stance w/arms behind
Slow look across from high R to high L
mf
From snow-capped moun - tain rang - es
16
mf
to o-ceans white with foam.
Look across from L to R
From the Col - o - ra - do plain to the
From the Col - o - ra - do plain to the
19
Cross fists front at chest
Open palms and drop
rock - y coast of Maine, this is the land we call home.
rock - y coast of Maine, this is the land we call home.
22
March
R
f
L
R
L
R palm over heart
Of thee I sing, A - mer - i - ca. My coun-try 'tis of
f
Of thee I sing, A - mer - i - ca. My coun-try 'tis of

25
March
R
L
R
L
thee. Of thee I sing, A - mer - i - ca,
thee. Of thee I sing, A - mer - i - ca,
28
R arm circle pan
from sea to shin - ing sea.
from sea to shin - ing sea.
Open stance facing R diagonal
31
A bit faster
mf
My coun - try 'tis of thee, sweet land of
mf
My coun - try 'tis of thee, sweet land of
34
lib - er - ty, of thee I sing.
lib - er - ty, of thee I sing.
37
R palm over heart
Land where my fa - thers died. Land of the
Land where my fa - thers died. Land of the

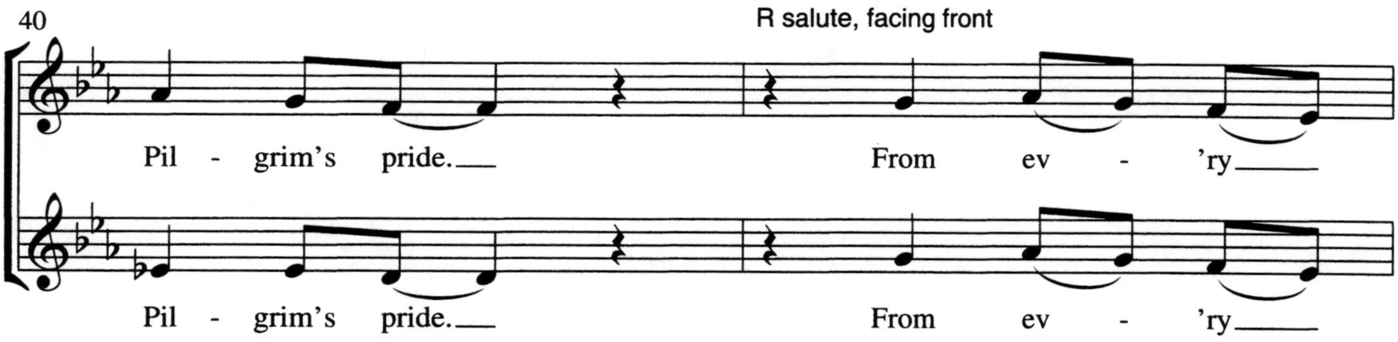
40
R salute, facing front
Pil - grim's pride. From ev - 'ry
Pil - grim's pride. From ev - 'ry

42
Push R up
cresc.
Drop to R
poco rit.
moun - tain - side let free - dom ring.
cresc.
moun - tain - side let free - dom ring.

45
Tempo I
DESCANT
March forward
R L R L
R salute
Push R up
A - mer - i - ca,
Tempo I
March in place
I.
R L R L
R palm over heart
Of thee I sing, A - mer - i - ca. My coun-try 'tis of
II.
Of thee I sing, A - mer - i - ca. My coun-try 'tis of

48
Drop to R
March back
R L R L
(end Descant, rejoin section)
of thee I sing.
March in place
R L R L
thee.
Of thee I sing, A - mer - i - ca,
thee.
Of thee I sing, A - mer - i - ca,
51
R arm circle pan
53
Divide into 4 groups
1. Salute 2.
from sea to shin - ing sea. From sea to
from sea to shin - ing sea. From sea to
54
3. 4.
Push R up and drop to R
R salute
shin - ing sea. From sea to
March
R L R L
shin - ing, of thee I sing, A - mer - i - ca.
57
Push R up and drop to R
both parts:
Open stance
rit.
Lift R up
ff
R salute
sea. A - mer - i - ca.
R L
ff
Of thee I sing, A - mer - i - ca.

NARRATOR 1:
American music is a mixture of the traditions of its people. Americans come from many cultures, and so does their music.

NARRATOR 2:
Our music reflects the history of America's people, America's trials, and America's growth.

NARRATOR 3:
The music of the American Indian includes legends, songs, and dances, rich in tradition and vital to our American heritage.

NARRATOR 4:
In the Navajo tribe, it was believed that if someone was sick, his spirit should journey to a holy place beyond the sacred mountain, where it could be healed.

NARRATOR 5:
But you could move most swiftly if you made this journey on a rainbow.

2. I MOVE SWIFTLY WITH THE RAINBOW

Words and Music by
SALLY K. ALBRECHT *and* **JAY ALTHOUSE**

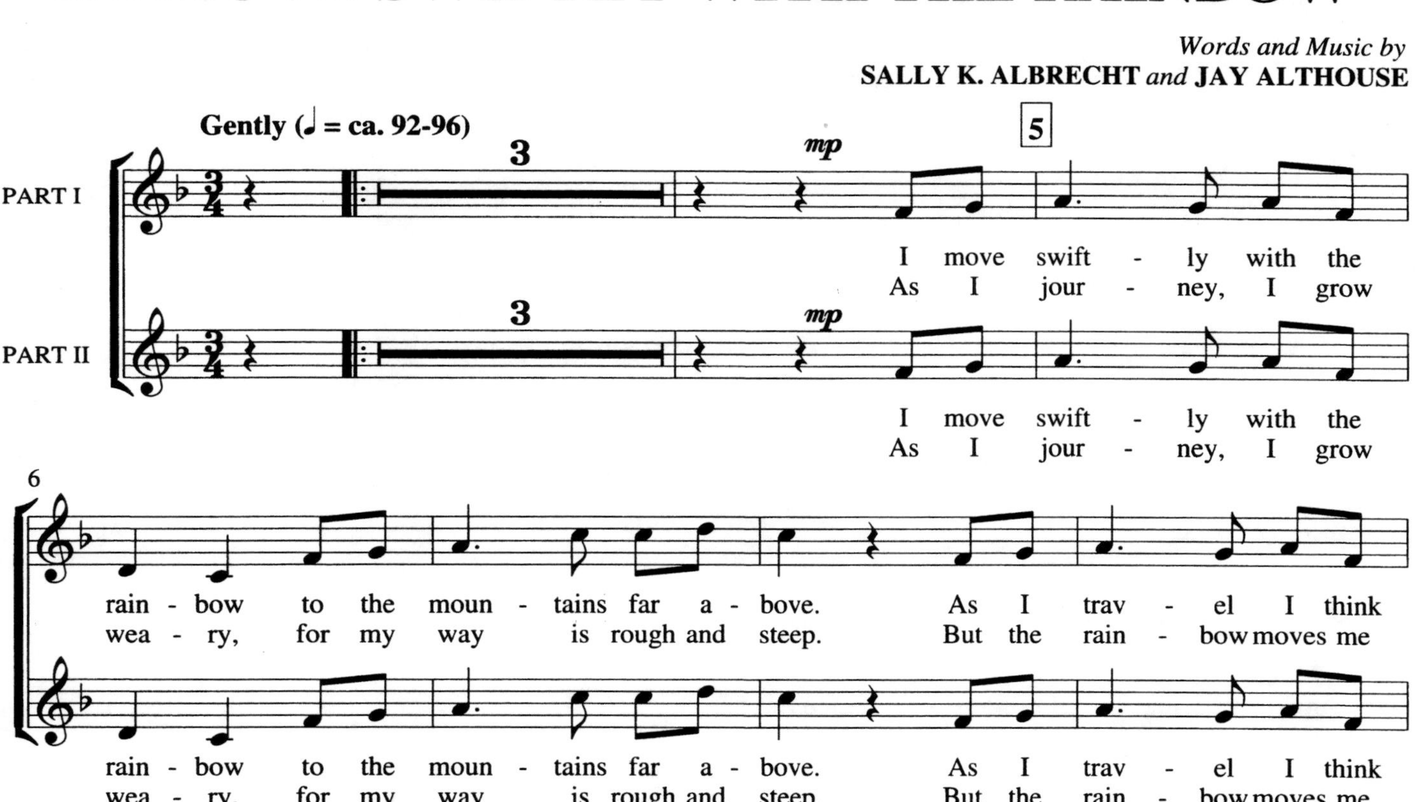

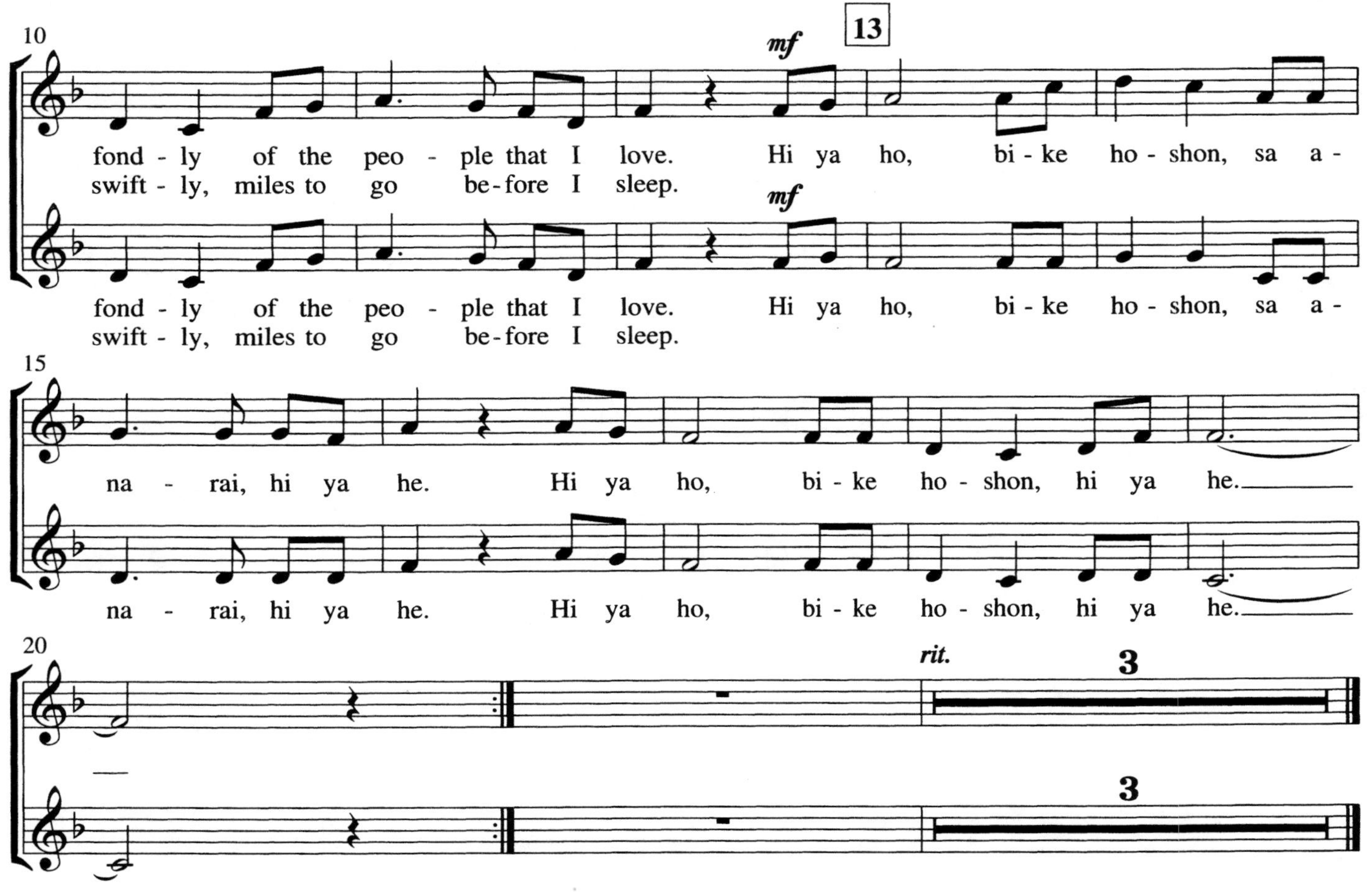

Translation/Pronunciation Guide
Hee yah hoh, (vocables)
bee-keh hoh-shawn, (happiness in all things)
sah ah-nah-reye, (life unending)
hee yah heh. (vocables)

NARRATOR 6:
Songs give people a common bond, which was especially important as America began to grow.

NARRATOR 7:
New songs were improvised and passed down. Songs of the common people—cowboys, farmers, railroad men, sailors, and lumberjacks.

NARRATOR 8:
This music was used to play games, to dance, to put children to sleep, to establish a working tempo.

NARRATOR 9:
These songs reflected the spirit of the common folk, and became known as American Folk Songs.

3. FOLK SONG MEDLEY

Arranged by
JAY ALTHOUSE

28
29
But first it bend - ed and then it broke.
tree. But first it bend - ed and then it broke.
32
mp
Thus did my love prove false to me.
mp
Thus did my love prove false to me.
37
rit.
Oo
The wa - ter is wide.
Oo
The wa - ter is wide.
42
Brightly (𝅗𝅥 = ca. 116)
mf
You
mf
You
46
Knee bends
down up down up etc.
ought to see my Cin - dy, she lives a - way down South. And
ought to see my Cin - dy, she lives a - way down South. And

50
Shimmer fingers at mouth
she's so sweet the hon-ey bees_ swarm a-round her mouth. Get a-long
she's so sweet the hon-ey bees_ swarm a-round her mouth. Get a-long
54
Scoop look R w/R above eyes
Scoop look L w/L above eyes
home, Cin-dy, Cin-dy, get a-long home, Cin-dy, Cin-dy. Get a-long
home, Cin-dy, Cin-dy, get a-long home, Cin-dy, Cin-dy. Get a-long
58
Scoop look front w/R above eyes
Clasp hands front
sub. p
home, Cin-dy, Cin-dy, I'll mar-ry you some-day. Get a-long
sub. p
home, Cin-dy, Cin-dy, I'll mar-ry you some-day. Get a-long
62
Scoop look R as before
Scoop look L
home, Cin-dy, Cin-dy, get a-long home, Cin-dy, Cin-dy. Get a-long
home, Cin-dy, Cin-dy, get a-long home, Cin-dy, Cin-dy. Get a-long
66
Scoop look front
cresc.
Clasp hands front
home, Cin-dy, Cin-dy, I'll mar-ry you some-
cresc.
home, Cin-dy, Cin-dy, I'll mar-ry you some-

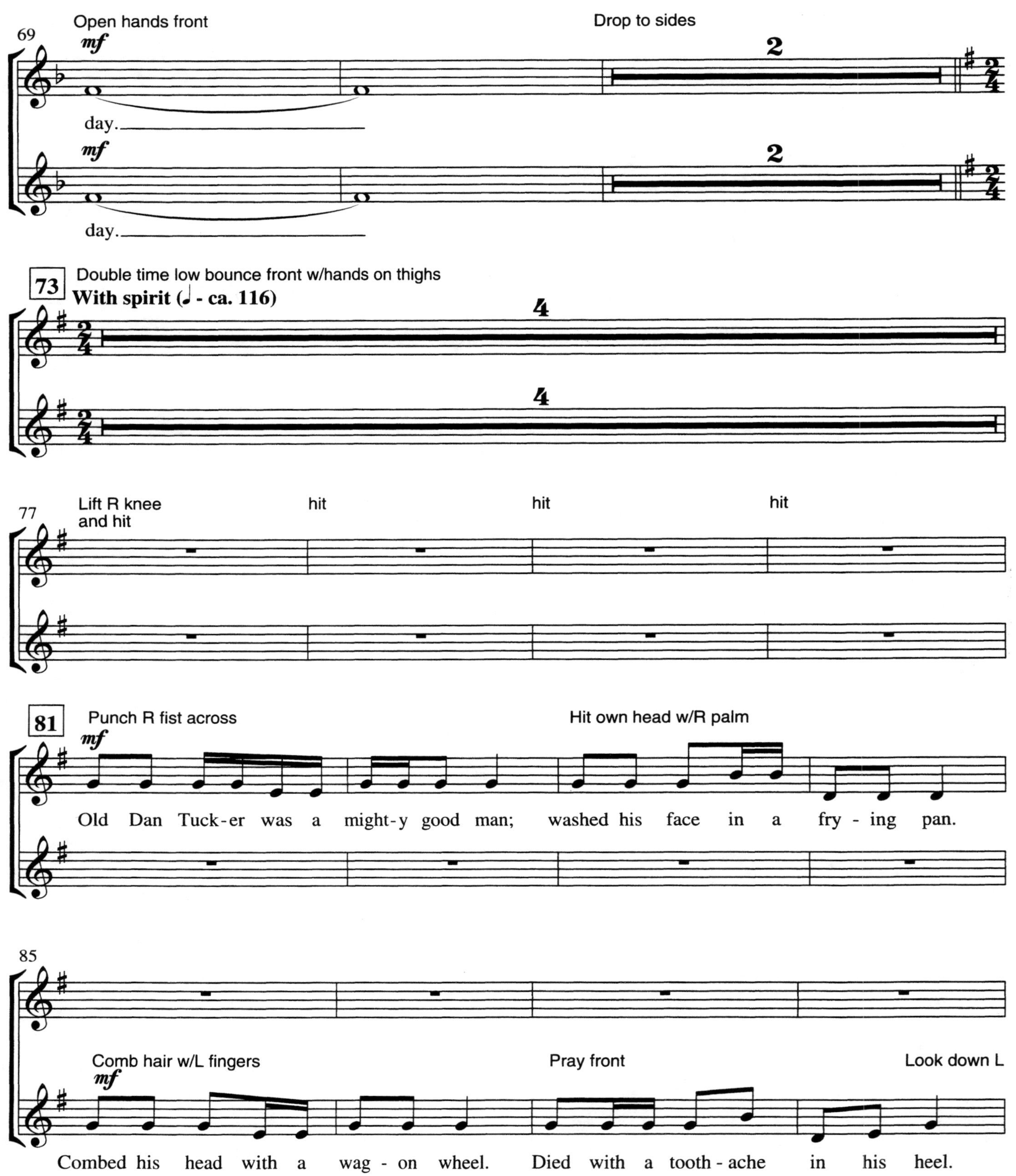
69
Open hands front
Drop to sides
mf
day.
mf
day.
2
2
73
Double time low bounce front w/hands on thighs
With spirit (♩ - ca. 116)
4
4
77
Lift R knee
and hit
hit
hit
hit
81
Punch R fist across
Hit own head w/R palm
mf
Old Dan Tuck-er was a might-y good man; washed his face in a fry - ing pan.
85
Comb hair w/L fingers
Pray front
Look down L
mf
Combed his head with a wag - on wheel. Died with a tooth - ache in his heel.

89
R index points out to R
Shake it 3x
mf
Get out the way, Old Dan Tuck-er. You're too late to get your sup-per.
Get out the way, Old Dan Tuck-er. You're too late to get your sup-per.
93
Flip R palm down
Flip L palm up
Fold arms front
Sup-per's o - ver and din-ner's cook-in', and Old Dan Tuck-er
Sup-per's o - ver and din-ner's cook-in', and Old Dan Tuck-er
96
Nod head front
97
Double time low bounce w/hands on thighs
3
stands there look - in'.
stands there look - in'.
100
Scoop R
L
R
L
105
Tilt clap
f
R
L
R
L
R lasso above 2x
Old Dan Tuck-er's back in town, swing-in' the la - dies all a - round.

109
Tilt clap
R
L
R
L
R lasso above 2x
First to the right and then to the left, then to the gal that
112
113
R index points to R
Shake it 3x
Get out the way, Old Dan Tuck-er. You're too late to
he loves best. Get out the way, Old Dan Tuck-er. You're too late to
116
Flip R palm down
Flip L palm up
get your sup - per. Sup-per's o - ver and din-ner's cook- in',
get your sup - per. Sup-per's o - ver and din-ner's cook- in', and
119
Fold arms
Open arms
Fists on waist
Old Dan Tuck - er stands there
Fold arms
Old Dan Tuck - er stands there
123
Scoop look R
Scoop look L
Lift R knee and hit 3x
R fist up
look - in'. Yes, sir!
look - in'. Yes, sir!

NARRATOR 10:

Spirituals were sometimes exultant, sometimes sad. They spoke of deliverance, of a journey to a better place, of seeking freedom, of hope for the future.

NARRATOR 11:

In the church, spirituals were sung in order to commune with God. There were songs of rejoicing, of prayer, of deliverance.

NARRATOR 12:

In the world outside of the church, African-Americans used spirituals to communicate. Lyrics were secret codes, telling of meetings or ways to escape.

NARRATOR 13:

Spirituals reflected years of African-American slavery, of being oppressed and in deep despair.

NARRATOR 14:

Yet, the lyrics ring of dignity, of power, of hope, faith, triumph, and rejoicing in the midst of those terrible dark times.

4. ELIJAH AND JOSHUA

Traditional Spirituals
Arranged by
SALLY K. ALBRECHT

With spirit (♩ = ca. 138-144)

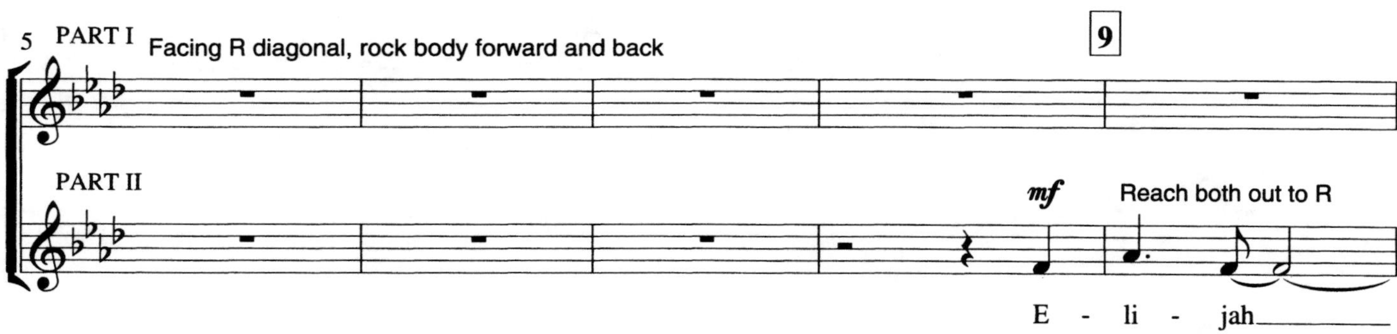

10
mf
Reach both out to R
Clasp and pull in
E - li - jah
Clasp and pull in
to L
and Josh - u - a.
14
Reach both out to L
Stomp and pull shoulders back
R L
and Josh - u - a.
17
Body rock
R to mouth L to mouth
Body rock
Shimmer jazz hands around face
E - li - jah rock, shout, shout. E - li - jah rock, com - in' up, Lord.
E - li - jah rock, shout, shout. E - li - jah rock, com - in' up, Lord.
21
Body rock
R to mouth L to mouth
Body rock
Push both jazz up to R
Snap 2x
E - li - jah rock, shout, shout. E - li - jah rock, com - in' up,
E - li - jah rock, shout, shout. E - li - jah rock, com - in' up,

25
Clasped hands circle from low R up ...
fp
cresc.
Lord
... and flip over to L and drop
Body rock
R to mouth
L to mouth
decresc.
E - li - jah rock, shout, shout. E - li - jah rock,
28
29
Reach L hand across to R and pull into chest
mp
Rock - a my soul in the bos - om of A - bra - ham.
shout, shout. Rock - a my soul in the bos - om of A - bra - ham.
31
w/R to L
Reach both up and cross at chest
cresc.
Rock - a my soul in the bos - om of A - bra - ham. Rock - a my soul in the
Rock - a my soul in the bos - om of A - bra - ham. Rock - a my soul in the
34
Stomp and shoulders
R L
mf
Clasped hands circle as before
cresc.
bos - om of A - bra - ham. Rock - a my soul.
mf Body rock
bos - om of A - bra - ham. E - li - jah rock,

37
R to mouth
L to mouth
shout, shout. E - li - jah rock, shout, shout.
40
Stand tall
R jazz palm front
L jazz palm front
Josh - ua fit the bat - tle of Jer - i - cho, Jer - i - cho,
Josh - ua fit the bat - tle of Jer - i - cho, Jer - i - cho,
43
Push both up and fall
Stand tall
Both jazz palms front
Jer - i - cho, Josh - ua fit the bat - tle of Jer - i - cho, and the
Jer - i - cho, Josh - ua fit the bat - tle of Jer - i - cho,
46
Push up
Push up 2x
decresc.
walls come tum - ba - lin' down, tum - ba - lin'
Push up
decresc.
walls come tum - ba - lin' down, tum - ba - lin'
49
Shimmer and drop
Slowly rise
down.
down.

52
53
Low pray
f
and the
f
Mime trumpet front
Then the lamb ram sheep-horns be - gan to blow,
55
Mime trumpet front
trum-pets be - gan to sound.
Stand tall
Then Josh - u - a com-mand-ed the
Then Josh - u - a com-mand-ed the
58
Push R fist up
peo - ple to shout, and the walls come tum - ba - lin' down,
Both jazz up
peo - ple to shout,
Both jazz up
walls come tum - ba - lin'
61
Push up 2x
decresc.
Shimmer and drop
tum - ba - lin' down.
decresc.
down, tum - ba - lin' down.
64
Slowly rise
2
66
Stand tall
mp
Josh - ua fit the bat - tle of
2
Low pray

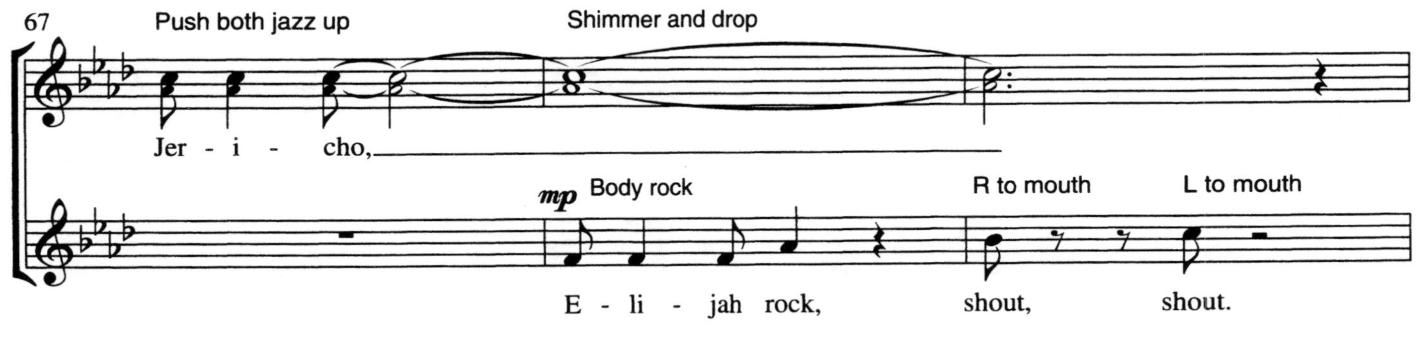
67
Push both jazz up
Shimmer and drop
Jer - i - cho,
mp Body rock
R to mouth
L to mouth
E - li - jah rock,
shout,
shout.

70
mf
cresc.
Josh - ua fit the bat - tle of
Jer - i - cho.
Low pray
mf Body rock
cresc.
E - li - jah rock,

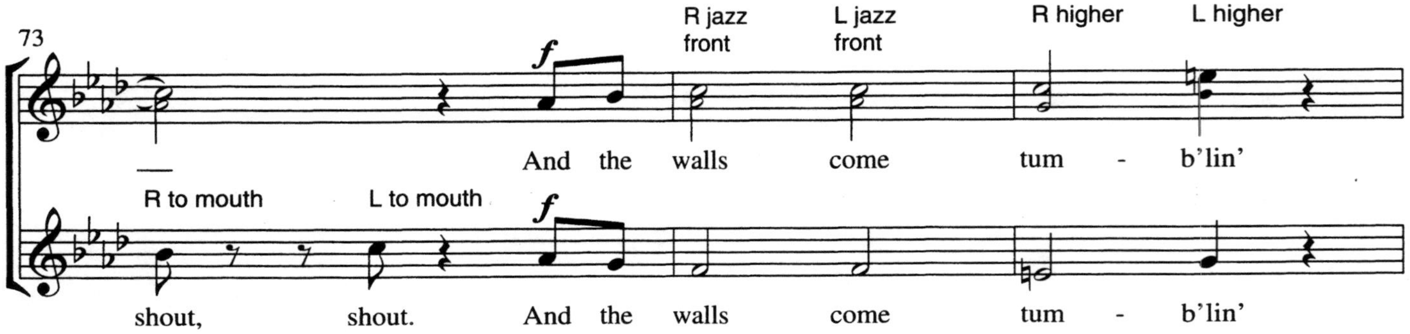
73
R jazz front
L jazz front
R higher
L higher
f
And the walls come tum - b'lin'
R to mouth
L to mouth
f
shout,
shout.
And the walls come tum - b'lin'

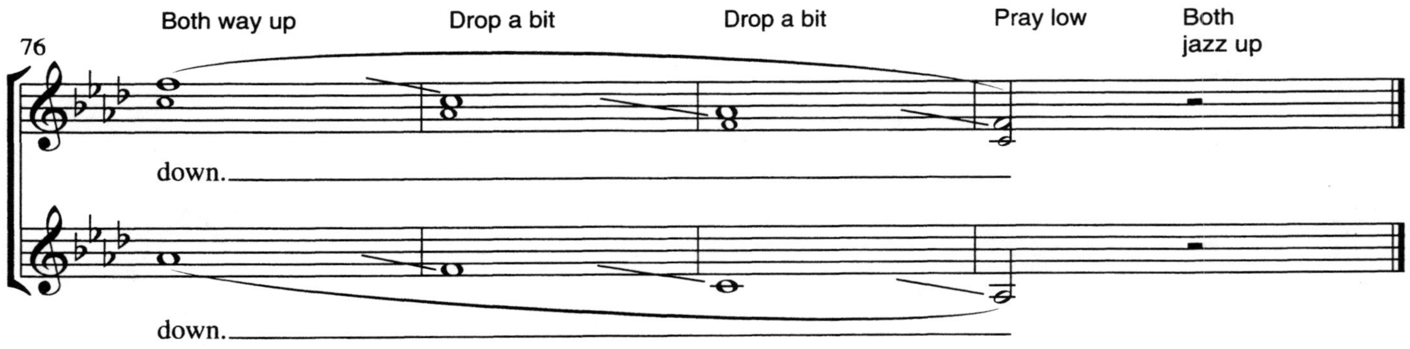
76
Both way up
Drop a bit
Drop a bit
Pray low
Both jazz up
down.
down.

NARRATOR 15:
In the early 1900s, a new kind of music appeared on the scene—Ragtime!

NARRATOR 16:
It was characterized by a syncopated or "ragged" melody over a steady "boom chick" bass line.

NARRATOR 17:
Ragtime music rang out from pianos in dance halls, clubs, theaters, and homes all across the country.

NARRATOR 18:
Plus, many of the best-selling rolls for player-pianos were ragtime. Composers Scott Joplin and "Jelly Roll" Morton popularized the style.

NARRATOR 19:
Ragtime music influenced future American musical styles, like Dixieland and jazz.

NARRATOR 20:
Here's a Dixieland-style version of Irving Berlin's famous song from 1911 called "Alexander's Ragtime Band." Listen for all the instruments!

5. ALEXANDER'S RAGTIME BAND

Arranged, with new words and music, by
SALLY K. ALBRECHT
and **JAY ALTHOUSE**

by **IRVING BERLIN**

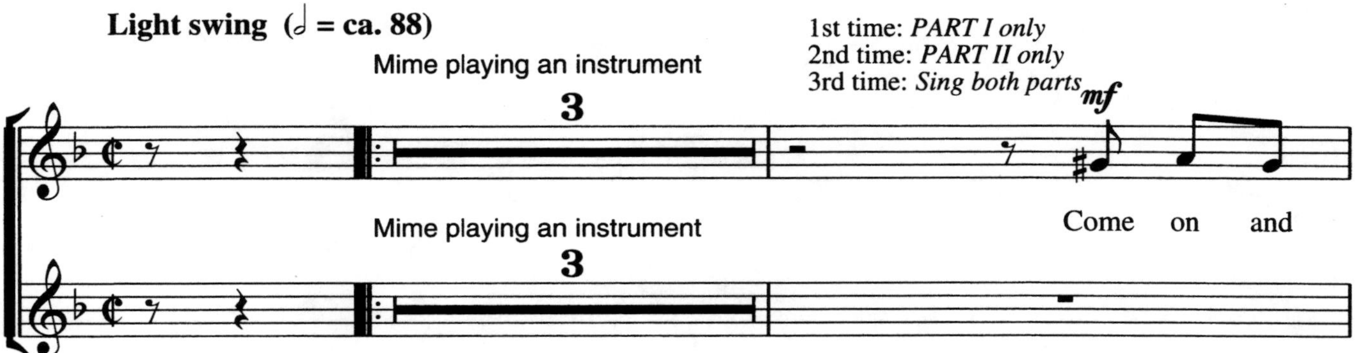

5
Scoop listen w/hand to ear:
R
L
R
hear, come on and hear Al - ex - an - der's Rag - time
Mime playing tuba – big R arm above, L arm curved front, big knee bends
mf
Oom - pah, oom - pah. Hear the tu - ba
8
L
R
L
Band. Come on and hear, come on and hear, it's the
Mime playing clarinet – hands front, L higher, lean forward and back
oom - pah - pah. The clar - i - nets, the clar - i - nets,
11
R
L
13
Hold "trumpet" front and tilt:
R
L
best band in the land. They can play a bu - gle call like you
Mime playing trumpet – hands at mouth, tilt R and L
3
doo-dle - oo, doo-dle - oo, the clar - i - nets. Ra - ta - ta - ta!
14
R
L
Salute w/R
nev - er heard be - fore, so nat - u - ral that you want to yell for more.
3
The bu - gle call. Ra - ta - ta - ta! The best of all.

both parts:
17
Stand tall
Punch R fist across to L
Pan R palm to R
Scoop front
That's just the best - est band what am, my hon - ey lamb. Come on a -
That's just the best - est band what am, my hon - ey lamb.
21
Place palm out:
R to R back
L to L back
R to R back
L to L back
long, come on a - long, let me take you by the hand, up to the
Mime playing trombone – L at mouth, R "slides" w/vocal line
Ah, ah. Hear the trom - bone, ah.
Shake jazz hands:
25
up
down
up
man, up to the man, who's the lead - er of the
Mime playing flute – hands to R of mouth, tilt R and L
Come hear the flute. Come hear the flute. Twee-dle- dee, twee-dle-
both parts:
Sway w/flat palms front:
28
down
29
R L R L R L
band. And if you care to hear the Swa - nee Riv - er played in
dee, come hear the flute. If you hear the Swa - nee Riv - er played in

NARRATOR 21:

Meanwhile, in New York City, Broadway was hitting its golden age.

NARRATOR 22:

After years of vaudeville and music hall entertainment, the "great white way" was developing its own kind of music.

NARRATOR 23:

Music and plot were intertwined. Dramatic stories were told through both dialogue and music lyrics.

NARRATOR 24:

The time was right as George M. Cohan came onto the scene in the early 1900s with these two hit Broadway songs.

6. A COHAN SALUTE

Arranged by
SALLY K. ALBRECHT

25
Bounce low 8x
I'm a real live Yan - kee Doo - dle, Made my name and fame and boo - dle,
I'm a real live Yan - kee Doo - dle, Made my name and fame and boo - dle,
29
Continue bounce, holding reins to the front
"Ride" pony facing stage L
Just like Mis - ter Doo - dle did, by rid - ing on a po - ny.
Just like Mis - ter Doo - dle did, by rid - ing on a po - ny.
33
Circle R arm hitting R thigh
37
Circle R lasso above head
41
March in place
R L R L R
I'm a Yan - kee Doo - dle Dan - dy, a Yan - kee
Ah, a Yan - kee Doo - dle, a Yan - kee

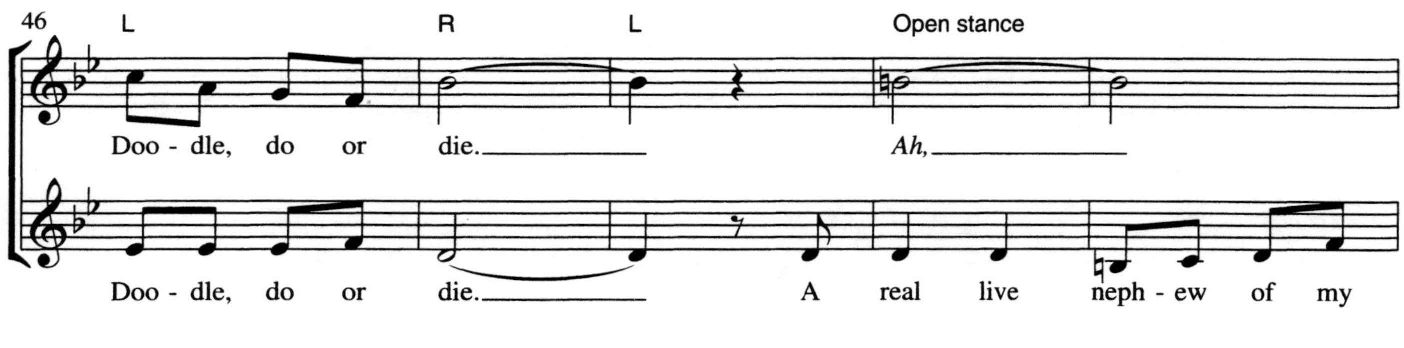
46
L
R
L
Open stance
Doo - dle, do or die.
Ah,
Doo - dle, do or die.
A real live neph - ew of my

51
R index point front
Baby rock
R
L
R
Un - cle Sam's,
Born on the Fourth of Ju - ly.
Un - cle Sam's,
Oh,
Fourth of Ju -

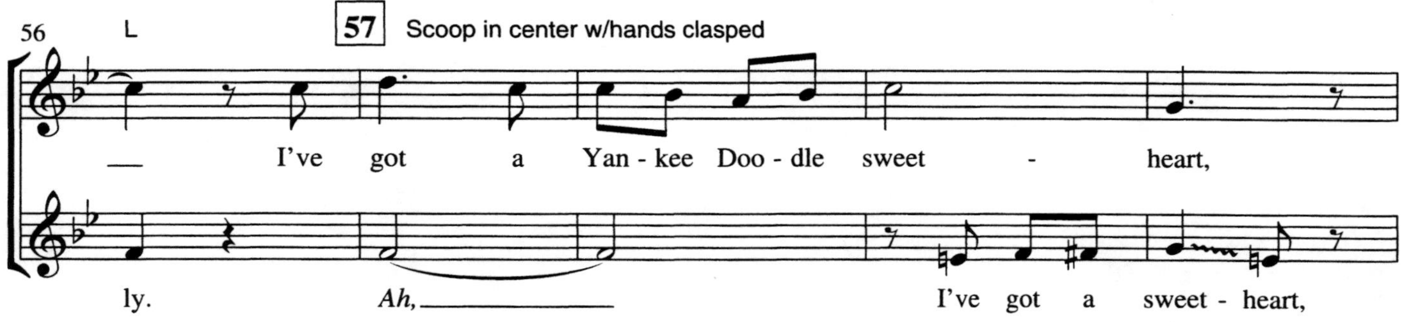
56
L
57
Scoop in center w/hands clasped
I've got a Yan - kee Doo - dle sweet - heart,
ly.
Ah,
I've got a sweet - heart,

61
Low (get kazoo)
She's (He's) my Yan - kee Doo - dle joy.
She's (He's) my Yan - kee Doo - dle joy.

65
"Yankee Doodle"
Hold kazoo like trumpet front. Use elbows and knees on piano rhythm
(Kazoos or "doot")
(Kazoos or "doot")
70
Low (put kazoo away)
I am a
I am a
75
Slowly stand
Yan - kee Doo - dle boy.
Yan - kee Doo - dle boy.
79
Face L diagonal, R lasso above as before
"You're a Grand Old Flag" by George M. Cohan
f
You're a
f
You're a
83
Face R diagonal w/R hand over heart
Push R out
grand old flag, you're a high fly - ing flag, And for - ev - er in
(mel.)
grand old flag, you're a high fly - ing flag, And for - ev - er in

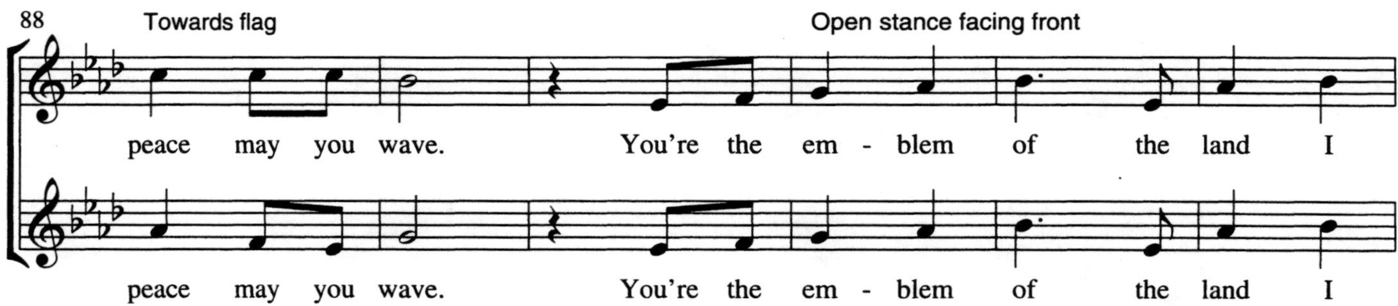
88
Towards flag
Open stance facing front
peace may you wave. You're the em - blem of the land I
peace may you wave. You're the em - blem of the land I

94
R salute
up down
love, The home of the free and the brave. Ev - 'ry
love, The home of the free and the brave. Ev - 'ry

99
R fist
up in up in up in up in
Palms flat to floor
(mel.)
heart beats true un - der Red, White, and Blue, Where there's nev - er a
(mel.)
heart beats true un - der Red, White, and Blue, Where there's nev - er a

104
Scoop into
group of friends
boast or brag. But should auld ac - quain - tance
Palms flat to floor
(mel.)
boast or brag. But should auld ac - quain - tance

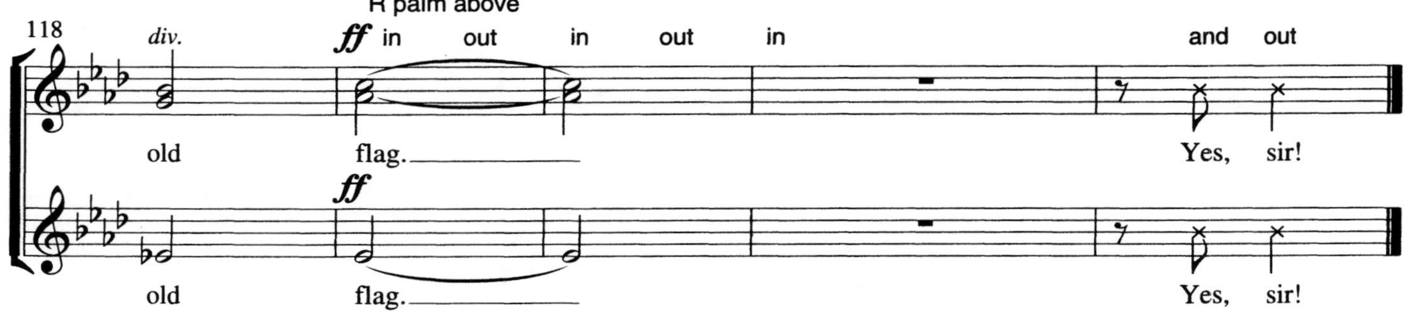

NARRATOR 25:

In the 1930s and 1940s, a new kind of music developed. Swing was king!

NARRATOR 26:

Big bands like those of Duke Ellington, Count Basie, Tommy Dorsey, and Woodie Herman played all over the world.

NARRATOR 27:

Instrumentalists like Louis Armstrong and singers like Ella Fitzgerald took this style of jazz to a new level.

NARRATOR 28:

Keep it steady. Keep it "laid back."

NARRATOR 29:

Keep tappin' those toes and poppin' those thumbs!

NARRATOR 30:

We're gonna "swing the night away!"

7. SWINGIN' THE NIGHT AWAY

Words and Music by
JAY ALTHOUSE

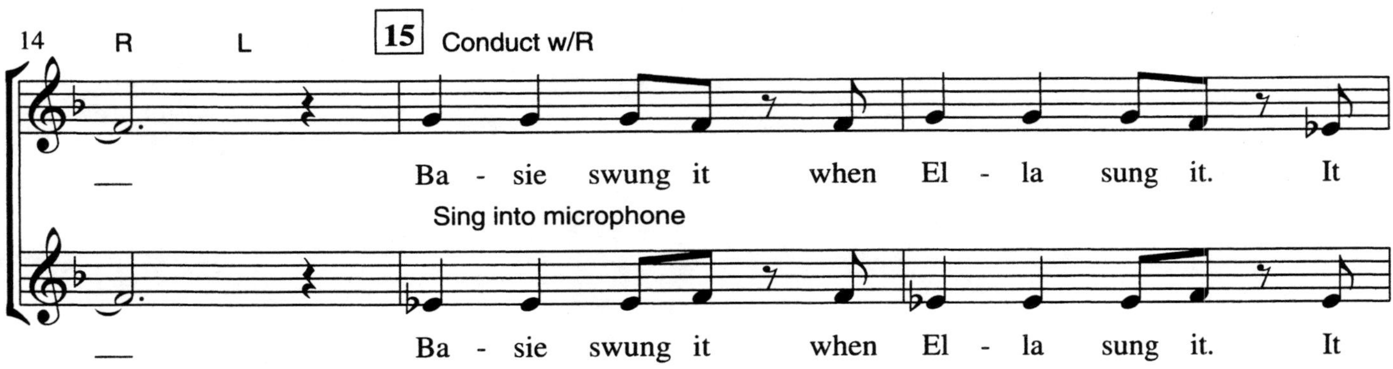
14
R
L
15
Conduct w/R
Ba - sie swung it when El - la sung it. It
Sing into microphone
Ba - sie swung it when El - la sung it. It

17
Finger digs in air
al - ways sound - ed fine.
Fans all dig it and cool cats gig it.
al - ways sound - ed fine.
Fans all dig it and cool cats gig it.

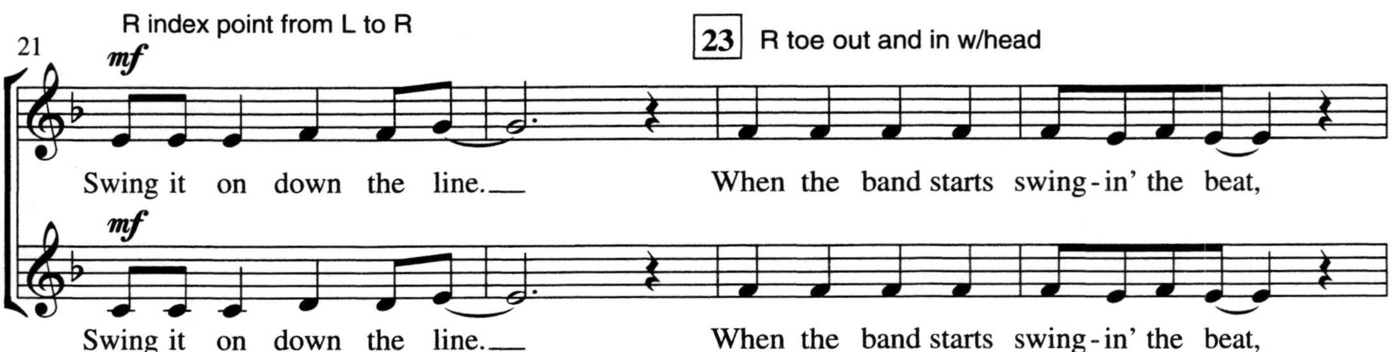
21
R index point from L to R
23
R toe out and in w/head
Swing it on down the line.
When the band starts swing - in' the beat,
Swing it on down the line.
When the band starts swing - in' the beat,

25
Palms flat to floor
makes me feel like tap - pin' my feet.
Noth - in' could be fin - er than
makes me feel like tap - pin' my feet.
Noth - in' could be fin - er than

NARRATOR 31:
"Country Music" originated in the southern United States in the mid 1920s. It has its roots in a combination of folk music, Celtic music, blues, and gospel music.

NARRATOR 32:
Jimmie Rodgers and the Carter Family are commonly acknowledged as the founders of country music.

NARRATOR 33:
Many different kinds of country music have developed and still exist today, including the "Nashville sound," bluegrass, traditional western cowboy songs, country swing, jug bands, and Cajun-style Zydeco music.

NARRATOR 34:
And most of the big names have appeared on one very famous show, which has been broadcast every Saturday night continuously from Nashville, Tennessee, since November 28, 1925.

NARRATOR 35:
What began as radio's "WSM Barn Dance" was renamed in 1927 as "The Grand Ole Opry."

NARRATOR 36:
From Roy Rogers to Gene Autry, from Johnny Cash to Ray Charles,...

NARRATOR 37:
...from Elvis Presley to Vince Gill, from Patsy Cline to Dolly Parton,...

NARRATOR 38:
...from Alison Krauss to Garth Brooks, from Willie Nelson to Reba McEntire, country music has produced an incredible string of famous entertainers.

8. MAKE MINE COUNTRY

Words and Music by
SALLY K. ALBRECHT *and* **JAY ALTHOUSE**

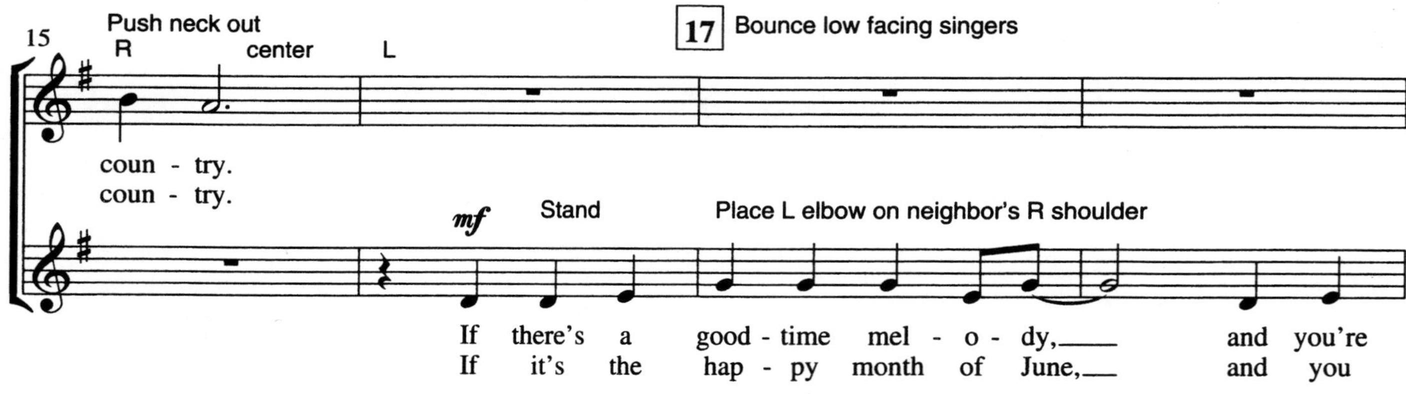

19
Stand tall
in the key of G and you need some har - mo - ny, make mine
need a song to croon, and you're look - in' for a tune, make mine
23
Stand
mf
25
Dip sway
R
L
Make mine coun - try, make mine
Push neck out
R
center
L
coun - try. Make mine coun - try, make mine
coun - try.
27
R
L
Bounce low
coun - try. A coun - try song can real - ly make me
coun - try. A coun - try song can real - ly make me
31
Get higher 3x
33
Dip sway
R
L
smile. Make mine coun - try, make mine
smile. Make mine coun - try, make mine

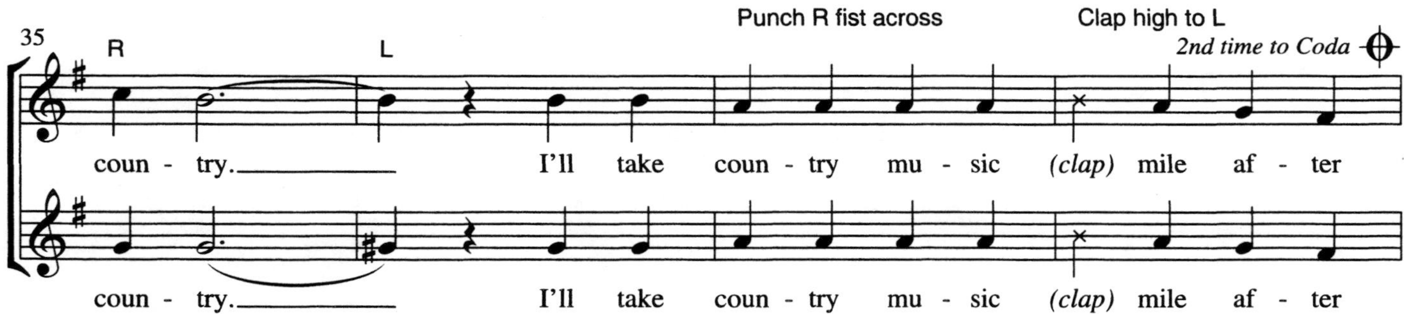
35
R
L
Punch R fist across
Clap high to L
2nd time to Coda
coun - try. I'll take coun - try mu - sic (clap) mile af - ter
coun - try. I'll take coun - try mu - sic (clap) mile af - ter

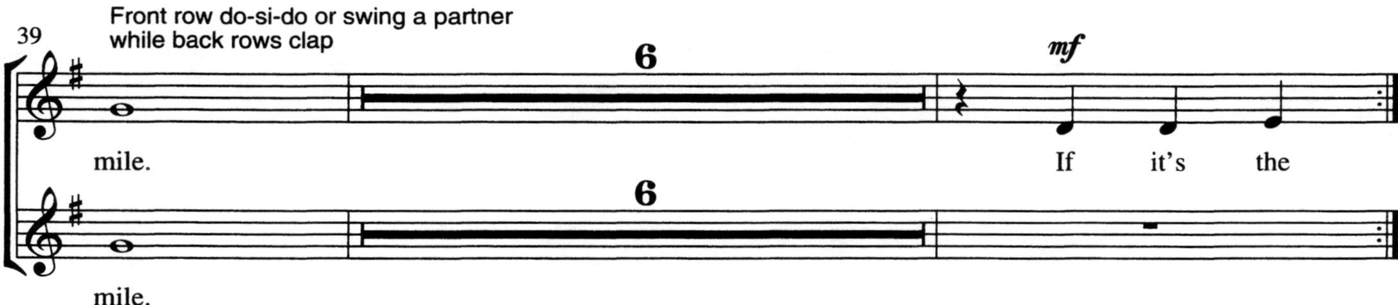
39
Front row do-si-do or swing a partner
while back rows clap
6
mf
mile. If it's the
6
mile.

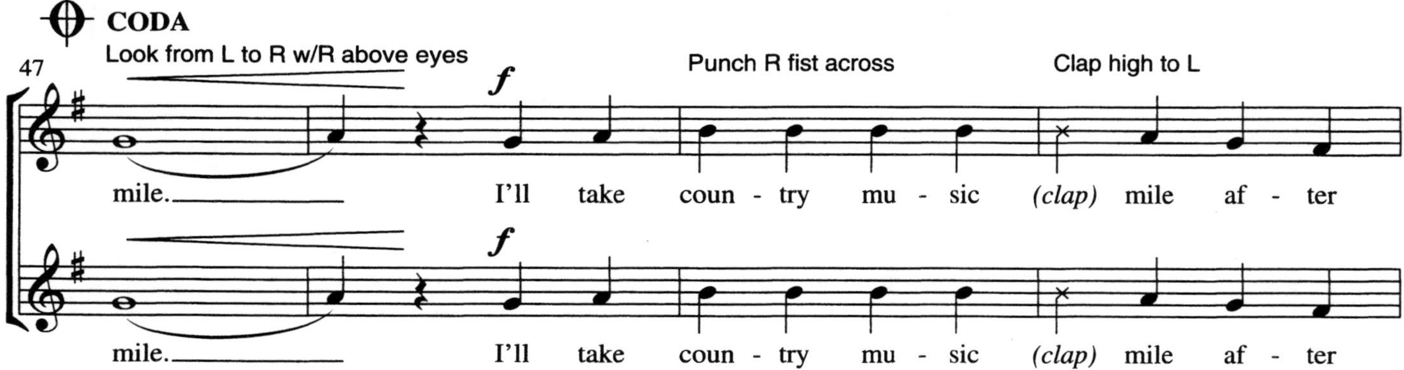
CODA
47
Look from L to R w/R above eyes
f
Punch R fist across
Clap high to L
mile. I'll take coun - try mu - sic (clap) mile af - ter
f
mile. I'll take coun - try mu - sic (clap) mile af - ter

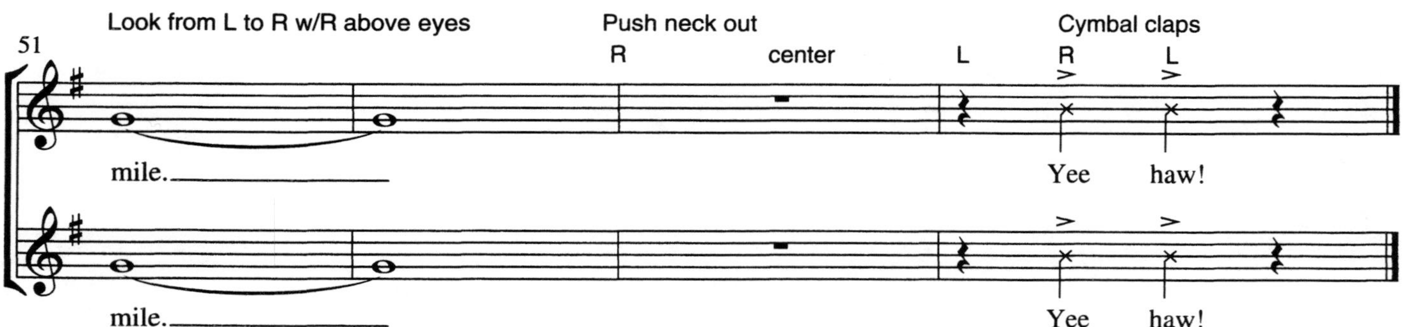
51
Look from L to R w/R above eyes
Push neck out
R
center
L
Cymbal claps
R
L
mile. Yee haw!
mile. Yee haw!

NARRATOR 39:
Since the mid 1950s, rock 'n' roll music has been one of the most popular forms of music in the world.

NARRATOR 40:
Alan Freed, a disc jockey from Cleveland, Ohio, is credited with coining the phrase "rock and roll."

NARRATOR 41:
Rock and roll combines elements of blues, soul, boogie-woogie, and jazz music.

NARRATOR 42:
The heart of rock and roll comes from the rhythm, which features a strong back beat, usually played on the snare drum.

NARRATOR 43:
So see how many song titles YOU recognize, at our "rock and roll party tonight!"

9. ROCK 'N' ROLL PARTY TONIGHT!

Words and Music by
JAY ALTHOUSE

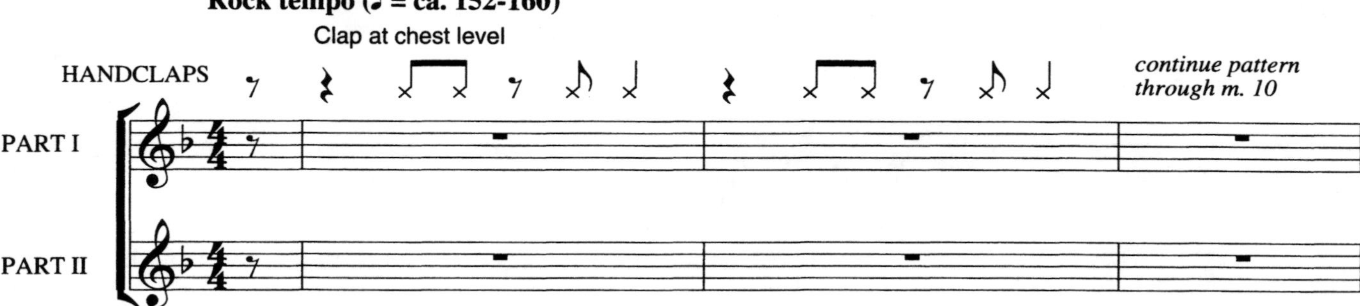

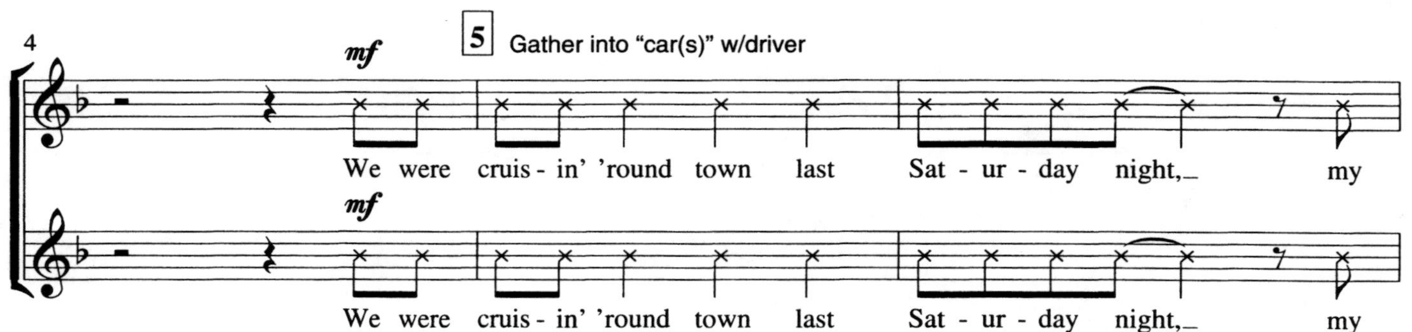

7
Walk out from "car(s)"
bud-dies and me; we were look-in' all right. We went to the dance, and when we
bud-dies and me; we were look-in' all right. We went to the dance, and when we

(Handclaps)
Freeze
Shake jazz hands to center
END HANDCLAPS
10
f
o-pened the door, we saw a rock 'n' roll par-ty on the dance floor. There was
o-pened the door, we saw a rock 'n' roll par-ty on the dance floor. There was

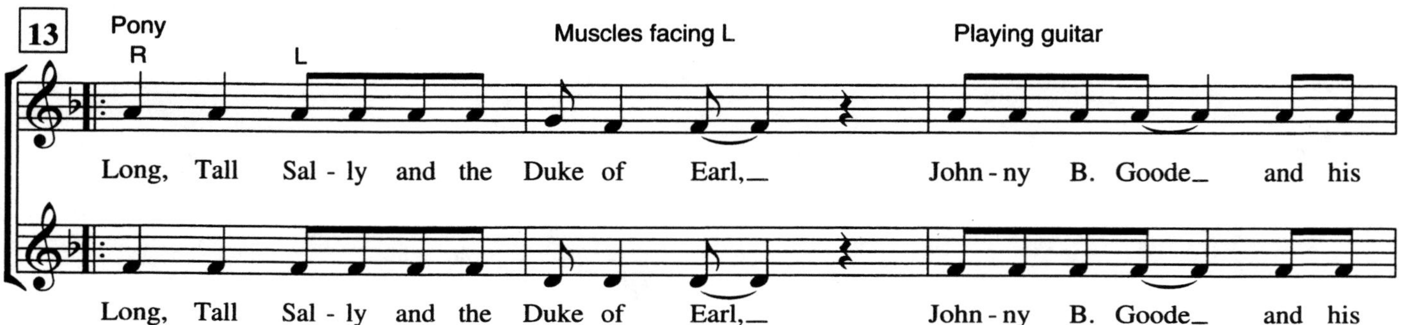
13
Pony
R
L
Muscles facing L
Playing guitar
Long, Tall Sal-ly and the Duke of Earl, John-ny B. Goode and his
Long, Tall Sal-ly and the Duke of Earl, John-ny B. Goode and his

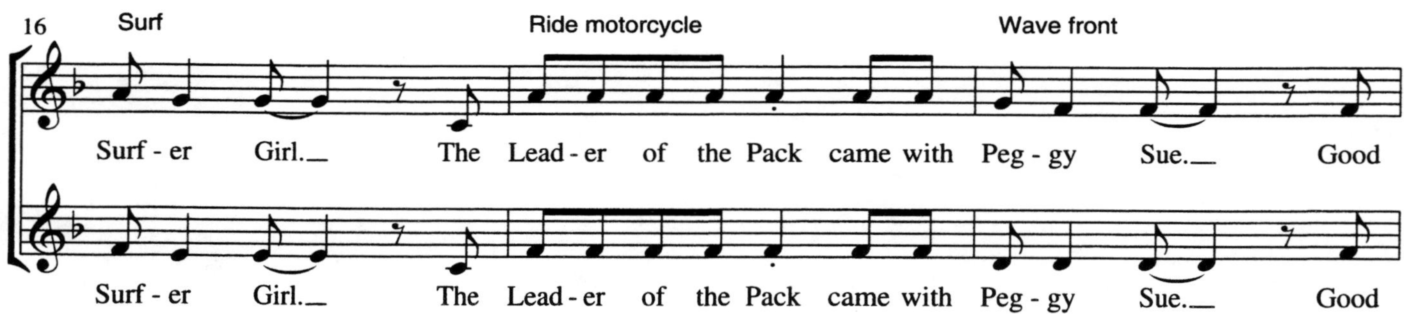
16
Surf
Ride motorcycle
Wave front
Surf-er Girl. The Lead-er of the Pack came with Peg-gy Sue. Good
Surf-er Girl. The Lead-er of the Pack came with Peg-gy Sue. Good

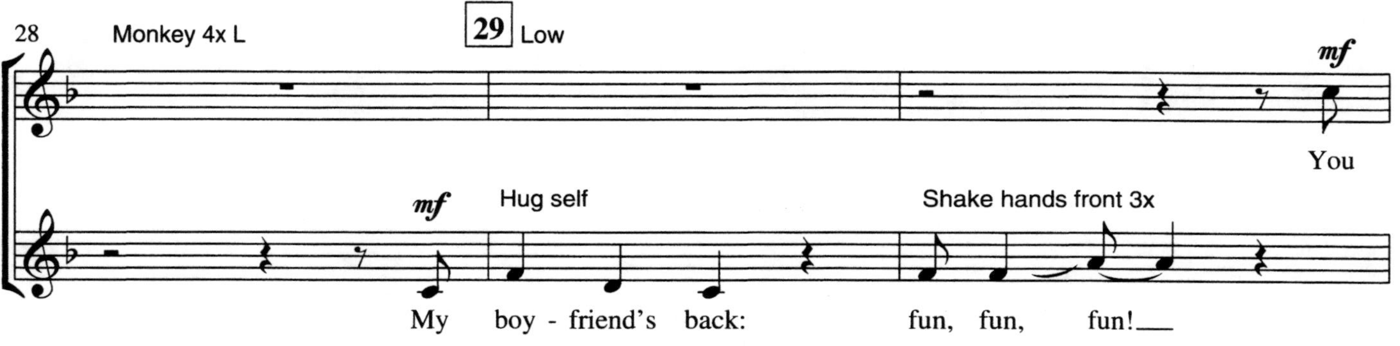

* Pronounced "Lou-ee, Lou-eye."

31
Fold arms – mad
Reach front
Low
can't hur - ry love, but you're still the one.
Low
Fists on waist – yell forward
How a - bout some R - E - S - P -

34
Palms out at sides
Boogie!
On - ly if you save the last dance for me.
Low
E - C - T?

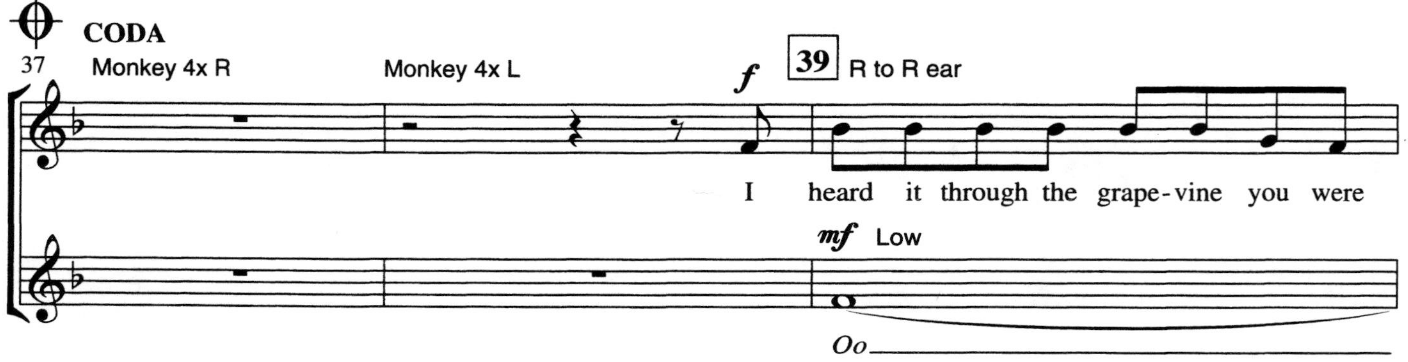
CODA
37
Monkey 4x R
Monkey 4x L
f
39
R to R ear
I heard it through the grape-vine you were
mf
Low
Oo

40
Swing hips and snap
R
L
R and hold
danc - in' in the street and toss - in' and a - turn - in' to the teen beat.
wah
oo
f
You

43
Low
f All low
One fine day I want to
Fists on waist
Hug self
talk too much; re-mem-ber walk-in' in the sand? One fine day I want to

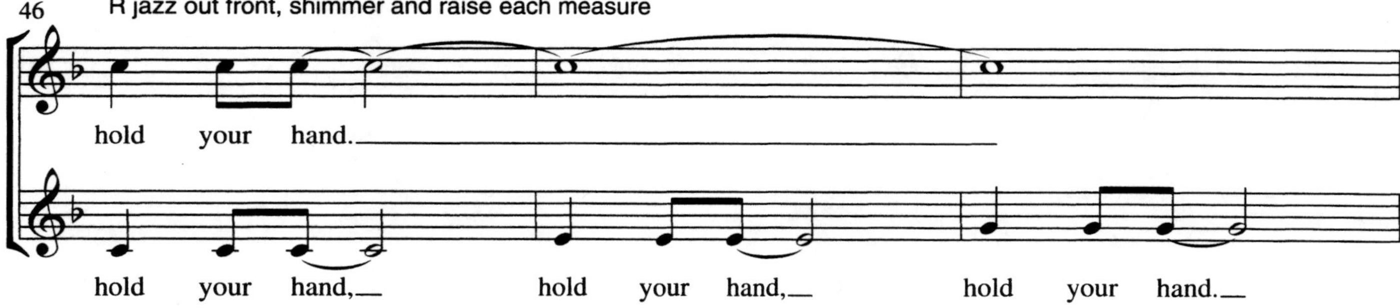
46
R jazz out front, shimmer and raise each measure
hold your hand.
hold your hand, hold your hand, hold your hand.

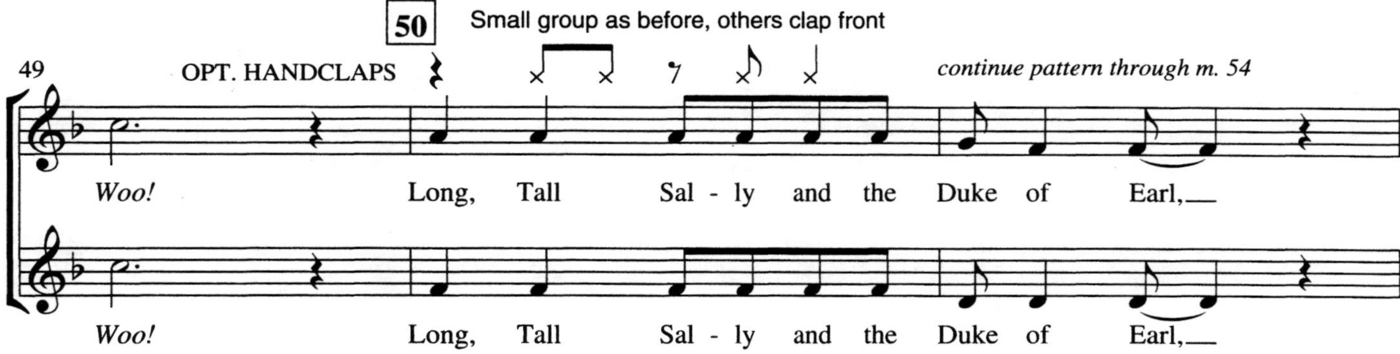
50
Small group as before, others clap front
49
OPT. HANDCLAPS
continue pattern through m. 54
Woo! Long, Tall Sal-ly and the Duke of Earl,
Woo! Long, Tall Sal-ly and the Duke of Earl,

52
John-ny B. Goode and his Surf-er Girl. The Lead-er of the Pack came with
John-ny B. Goode and his Surf-er Girl. The Lead-er of the Pack came with

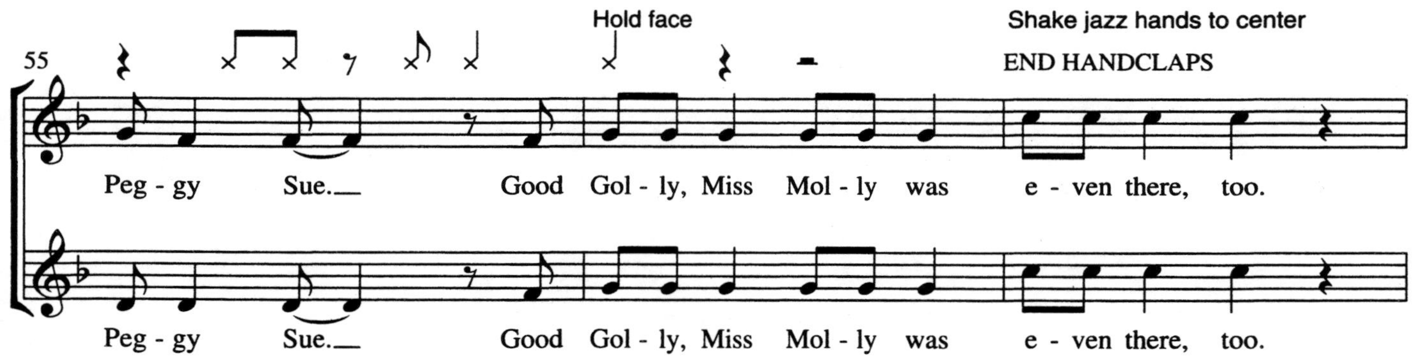
55
Hold face
Shake jazz hands to center
END HANDCLAPS
Peg - gy Sue.__ Good Gol - ly, Miss Mol - ly was e - ven there, too.
Peg - gy Sue.__ Good Gol - ly, Miss Mol - ly was e - ven there, too.

58
Low
R flat palm forward
Look out now,__ 'cause it's
Pony
R
L
Hitch 4x w/R
Low
Hey, hey Pau - la and Lou - ie, Lou - ie.__

61
Cry to R w/R
Swing hips and snap
R
L
R
L
Ju - dy's turn to cry. Come on ev - 'ry - bod - y, it's a rock 'n' roll par - ty.

64
Low
All swing hips and snap
R
L
Come on ev - 'ry - bod - y, it's a
Swing hips and snap
R
L
R
L
Come on ev - 'ry - bod - y, it's a rock 'n' roll par - ty. Come on ev - 'ry - bod - y, it's a

NARRATOR 44:

The history of American music is truly varied and amazing.

NARRATOR 45:

Each style is unique in its own way, but is rooted in the history of the American people.

NARRATOR 46:

New styles are still being developed. In the late 20th and early 21st century, rap and hip-hop have been embraced by the American music scene.

NARRATOR 47:

From Native American Indian chants to traditional folk songs,...

NARRATOR 48:

... from inspirational spirituals to hot New Orleans ragtime,...

NARRATOR 49:

... from jazzy swing to kickin' Broadway 2-beat,...

NARRATOR 50:

... from Nashville's Grand Ole Opry to the Detroit Motown Sound,...

ALL:

... America has developed a sound all its own.

10. FINALE: OF THEE I SING, AMERICA!

18
Drop to R
March back
R L R L
(end Descant, rejoin section)
of thee I sing.
March in place
R L R L
thee.
Of thee I sing, A - mer - i - ca,
thee.
Of thee I sing, A - mer - i - ca,
21
R arm circle pan
23
Divide into 4 groups
1. Salute 2.
from sea to shin - ing sea. From sea to
from sea to shin - ing sea. From sea to
24
3. 4.
Push R up and drop to R
R salute
shin - ing sea. From sea to
March
R L R L
shin - ing, Of thee I sing, A - mer - i - ca.
27
Push R up and drop to R
both parts:
Open stance
rit.
Lift R up
ff
R salute
sea. A - mer - i - ca.
R L
ff
Of thee I sing, A - mer - i - ca.

Of Thee I Sing!
A Celebration of America's Music
for 2-Part Choirs
by Sally K. Albrecht and Jay Althouse
Recording Produced by Alan Billingsley
Alfred